MW00324947

I just finished reading and HIGHLY enjoyed *Running Away from the Circus*! At times while reading I would laugh out loud and my wife would say, "What is so funny?" so I would explain what had made me laugh so hard.

> — **Kenzia Drake, St. Pius X Seminary**

I LOVED this book! First of all, the subject matter is so different; from Nove's life in the circus to his study in the seminary to the conflict between these different callings.

> — **Anne Boone Johnson, Retired Professor of International Education, Univ. of W. Florida**

I'll start by saying how much I enjoyed reading Nove's "life story." He writes well and with a real sense of humor, so it's quite hard not to enjoy the book.

> — **Dr. Joseph Sheley, President Emeritus of California State University, Stanislaus and author of *Preordained***

I've known Nove since he was a little kid when I worked on his uncle's circus. His circus and carnival material captures the times authentically and presents a much-needed, positive perspective on Circus and Carnival folk.

> — **Chester Cable, "The Man with the Educated Feet" co-owner, LA Circus and Guinness World Record holder**

RUNNING AWAY FROM THE CIRCUS

CONFESSIONS OF A CARNIE KID
(WHO TRIED TO BECOME A PRIEST)

NOVE MEYERS

For Priscilla. Enjoy

atmosphere press

© 2021 Nove Meyers

Published by Atmosphere Press

Cover design by Beste Miray

No part of this book may be reproduced without permission from the author except in brief quotations and in reviews.

atmospherepress.com

TABLE OF CONTENTS

PART IV - SMILE, JESUS LOVES YOU

PART V - AFTER THE FALL

EPILOGUE

For My Dad
The Original Nove

PART I

OF CIRCUSES AND SACRAMENTS

NEAR MISSES

My grandmother could fly.

Every night she flew from one slim trapeze bar to the other, twisting, somersaulting, gracefully floating through the air as though gravity itself had been suspended. Thirty feet above the sawdust-covered circus ring she flew—no net.

She would briefly descend to the ground. When she rose again, the sequins on her winged costume shimmered in the spotlight. Slowly rising, gently spinning. At the apex, her butterfly wings fell away like a chrysalis in reverse. As the wings fluttered softly back to earth, the crowd gasped its astonishment, realizing that she was held aloft only by her teeth, gripping the end of a small metal and leather device— the Iron Jaw.

There, hanging by her teeth, she began twirling, slowly at first in tight spins. Then faster, making wider arcs. As she spun round, she gradually descended back to the ground amid the roars of applause.

Dollie Mae LaStarr was the queen of the circus, its prima donna.

But Dollie Mae wasn't the only trapeze artist using the Iron

Jaw. It was the current fascination: the one act that most impressed the crowds. It's what they came to the circus for—more than the jugglers, the clowns, even the elephants. And each of the prima donnas from competing circuses tried to outdo the others.

It was almost the essence of the circus, to go beyond where anyone else had been; to be more elaborate, riskier, more daring; to exceed the hype on the posters the advance men had plastered on barns announcing that the circus was coming to town.

Dollie Mae had an idea. *What if? What if, instead of hanging by her teeth, she hung by her knees from a trapeze ring and inverted the Iron Jaw. And what if, hanging from that ring, she grasped one end of the Jaw in her own teeth while the other end held something else: her young child, barely more than a toddler? What if that child, not she, would spin, protected from harm only by its own mother's clinched teeth?*

No one could compete. No one tried. No one even dared. And the crowds swelled, night after night after night.

Until the circus tent filled to overflowing.

Until the night the leather stretched a bit too much.

Until her child plunged to the sawdust thirty feet below.

The crowd shrieked its horror and Dolly Mae hung midair, forgotten, as Granddad and his circus workers rushed to the small bundle lying motionless in the ring.

And my story could have ended right here: the first of the *what if*s that seem to string themselves together to direct a life along its way—or not.

***

Our family circus had been started by my great-grandfather, Andrew Jackson Richards. He left Georgia after the war that was called "civil," although it's hard to consider any war that. It's not entirely clear how he started, as family lore differs. We do know that by the early twentieth century his three sons—Henry, Franco, and Wesley—were operating circuses based out of a five-hundred-acre ranch in Pipe Creek, Texas, sometimes partners, sometimes competitors.

My mother was born into this circus family in 1920, the year that women gained the right to vote, and the rest of America lost the right to drink. Her daddy owned the circus and named his daughter after his elephant, Maxine. According to her daddy, Mother wasn't born at all. His wife loved tamales and he frequently bought her some from a roving vendor. And one day, wrapped in a husk among the tamales, they found Mother. That's what her daddy had said. And that's why he called her his little "senorita."

***

The child lay still as its father picked it up; but, as he cradled it in his arms, the baby opened its eyes and began to cry. It didn't die, but Dollie Mae's Iron Jaw act did. The incident occurred when my mother was two or three years old. Usually, when she told the story, it was she herself who fell, but sometimes it was her brother. Possibly, Mother was unsure herself. Her brother always suffered from back trouble, so it might have been him. But then again, the earliest photo that I have of Mother shows her with Grandmother in a trapeze costume.

In a certain way, it doesn't really matter. It was a circus, after all. In a circus, things get embellished—like the size of the elephant, or the wonders promised by the sideshow marquees—and twisted, like the spins of a trapeze artist as she flies through the air, or the location of the pea under a walnut shell. And the years and the decades of tale telling itself take their toll on an octogenarian mind.

But one fact that cannot be denied, one "what if" that did and one that didn't happen. We still have the broken Iron Jaw, rusted metal and torn leather; and two more generations of a circus family have lived, and outlived, the circus itself.

And *"what if"* one of them would want to join not the circus but the Catholic priesthood? What would God think of that?

***

This is where I come in. The one who thought he wanted to be a priest? Yeah, that was me. I first dipped my toe in the center ring of life smack dab in the center of the twentieth century. Unlike my mother, though, I wasn't born directly onto a working circus; there was no talk of tamale wrappers, virgin births, or other distractions. I came the regular way, with a doctor and a hospital room, as far as I know, although I have to take others' word for it, as I was quite young at the time. And it is true that several of the congratulatory cards in the baby book that Mother put together clearly show an infant being hauled in by a smiling stork, so I can't be certain.

Mine may have been a regular gestation and birth, but my childhood was hardly your boy scout path to merit badges sort of a thing, as we shall see. My family followed its own rules, or lack thereof, marking my earliest memories. And that's before we even begin to get to the God stuff. Let's start with a few early stories to show you what I mean.

***

"I don't want my mommy to burn up like paper!" I hear my three-year-old lungs scream their first full sentence. I knew that my mommy was always cold, even in California, and on that particular day, she'd backed herself up to our gas fireplace while chatting with Uncle Rusty, the brother she had raised from infancy by herself after both her parents had died. Rusty was home on furlough from the Korean War and was still wearing his uniform. Standing in front of the flames gently rising from the faux aspen logs, they looked like a picture that Norman Rockwell might have painted for *Life Magazine*.

Fake logs, real flame. Mommy must have backed a bit too close to the flames, which couldn't resist reaching out for the thin fabric she was wearing. I smelled it first, like paper burning, before I saw the flames licking at the hem of her sundress.

That's when I screamed.

"Mac, you're on fire," her brother yelled as he grabbed her, trying to extinguish the flames with his bare hands.

Dad heard the commotion and rushed to the living room. "Hold still, dammit," he commanded, as he grabbed Mommy and threw her to the ground, rolling her in the oval rug which covered the floor in front of the fireplace. Then he flung himself on top of her and held her until he was sure the flames were out. After a couple of minutes, he unrolled the rug and gently picked her up. Modesty took a back seat as he peeled off what was left of her dress, leaving her just in a bra and slip, until my uncle grabbed a blanket off the couch.

I stood there frozen, as if my feet were glued to that living room floor.

Mommy was clearly shaken, and a dress short of a full wardrobe, but suffered no permanent damage from the incident. After she had recovered, she held me tight and told me what a brave boy I was.

The worst injuries, though, were to my uncle's hands, which probably should have been treated at the ER but weren't. The small white scars there served as a lifetime reminder of this near-miss that could have changed my life forever, just about the time it was getting started good, another *"what if."*

My reward for saving Mommy from the fire was a tricycle. She was a beauty. I see myself standing on the sidewalk outside the metal gate that leads into our front yard, or what would have been the front yard, were the space not dominated by an unused koi pond guarded by hideous gargoyles that a previous owner had installed.

"Some assembly required," the box must have said. I watched wide-eyed as Dad removed the parts from the trunk of his 1950 Lincoln and used a wrench to transform the oddly shaped metal into the Harley Davidson of tricycles. It was bigger than I was: a shimmery copper color with contrasting stripes. The pedals were chain driven, like a bicycle, not mounted on the front wheel like a regular trike. After he tightened the last nut, greased the chain, and checked all the fittings like a NASCAR mechanic, Dad sat me on the seat and showed me how to grip the handlebars, ready to teach his first son how to ride.

My short legs dangled in the air, a few inches of nothingness between them and the pedals of my marvelous new toy.

As Dad headed toward the garage, mumbling something about needing some "goddamn blocks," a young stranger walked up to me.

"Hi. I'm Tommy. Is this your trike?" She was tall, at least compared to me, and had blue eyes like mine; and her brown hair was cut in a bob.

I muttered a "yes."

And again, "My name is Tommy. What's yours?'

An inquisitive look met my answer, "Engineer," the nickname that I had acquired because of my fetish for railroad trains.

"What kind of a name is that?"

"I like trains."

It satisfied her.

"Can I try out your trike? You can come along." Without quite waiting for an answer, she helped me off the trike, told me to stand on the back and put my arms around her waist. She took the controls, and away we went, towards her house, half a block away. We turned around in the driveway of her white stucco house, nearly identical to its next-door neighbor, and returned to my gate. So now I had my trike, which my dad fixed so my feet could reach the pedals, and a playmate. Or my first girlfriend, a take-charge older woman, her five years to my not-quite-four.

We hung out for a couple of years before my family moved from Albany to Fairfield to be closer to my dad's job. I missed Tommy after we moved and wanted to go see her when we visited my aunt, who had rented our previous house. But by then, the family had moved. Or maybe I got confused and knocked on the wrong door. Well, she probably already had another boyfriend by then anyway.

***

Nearly being roasted herself had little to do with it, but Mommy hated smoking—and Dad needed it. He was a two-pack-a-day Camel man. He bought them by the carton and would go through a carton a week easy, turning two hundred cancer sticks into a houseful of butt-filled ashtrays. My rough calculation is that he managed to choke on half a million of 'em before they finally got him, give or take.

I was on Dad's side. I probably started smoking because of the smoke rings. Dad would blow his smoke rings at me as a toddler—not as perfect or sexy as the sultry broads in the movies, but they intrigued me. I wanted those smoke rings. Got so he couldn't light up with me around that I didn't pester him, getting right in his face. A man has few enough solitary pleasures without a two-year-old hounding him every time he tries to relax.

And, like the "first fix is free" from the drug dealer they warn you about, I didn't quit with smoke rings. My dad was putting the thing in his mouth, and I wanted to do that too. I'm sure he tried to put me off. Any good parent would. But, as any parent also knows, two-year-old's have a penchant for perseverance. I kept crawling into his lap and trying to grab the hot end and he kept saying no, until he didn't one day. He probably figured, *What the hell. I'll let the kid try it. That'll fix him.* He showed me how to hold the cigarette and put it to my lips.

My eyes might have been watering, but I was sittin' pretty.

And I didn't let up.

It may have been my cigarette-hating mother who suggested he teach me how to inhale. "Teach him how to suck it in, Sweetheart. That's bound to cure him."

Once again, it didn't.

I was addicted to the whole experience. I didn't even object when they were out of Camels, and Dad occasionally got a pack of Chesterfields or Lucky Strikes. I hear that I liked the look of the Lucky Strike packaging better anyway. This was before the tobacco industry got the idea to market to kids directly, using cartoon characters such as "Joe Camel." If I'd have been going to preschool, I'm sure I would have impressed all the ladies.

Now I don't personally remember any of this and would doubt that it had ever happened, were it not for the photographs. Mommy, the nightclub photographer, captured everything on film. Her first effort, when I was a month old, featured me in my "birthday suit." She printed it out as a Christmas card with "Merry Christmas, Happy New Year" scrawled across my infant torso leaving nothing to the imagination. The camera even caught me mid-pee.

At first, everybody thought my smoking was "cute," or "precocious." But my dad was already experiencing coughing fits some mornings, a harbinger of his eventual demise, and Mommy started to get worried. Finally, she put her foot down. It was the morning of my third birthday. I had asked my dad for a birthday smoke when Mommy said enough was enough.

"No more smoking for you. It's not good for you. It's not good for your daddy either, but he's a grown-up."

"Mommy," she claimed I said, "if I can have just one more cigarette now, on my birthday, I won't ever ask again."

The photo from that day shows me, wearing my train

engineer overalls, puffing away. I've got the cigarette held between my second and third fingers up to my lips, smoke curling from the business end. I never asked for another cigarette and never took up smoking again. To date, I've lived a decade longer than my dad managed to, something that may not have happened if I hadn't snuffed out that last butt on my third birthday.

***

It's two years later: a new house in a new town. But the burning smells stayed with me. So, when I got a whiff of smoke coming from the direction of our garage, I rushed through the house. I was just about to step onto the cold garage floor when I froze, one foot still in the air and my hands gripping the door frame. Not ten feet away from me, Mommy and Uncle Rusty were huddled over the concrete wash sink meticulously burning stacks of crisp twenty-dollar bills. Like newspaper used for kindling in a fireplace, these little green portraits of Andrew Jackson would first gently blacken, as if contemplating their fate, before curling and bursting into flame. They then became a shadow of their former selves, the consistency of butterfly wings. It was a slow, deliberate process, as they burned them, one by one, to reduce those stacks of twenties to an indistinguishable ash heap, which they then washed down the sink drain. They were talking in hushed tones, and I couldn't make out what they were saying. The concrete sink they were standing at was just a few feet from the door of the darkroom Dad had built for Mommy to use as a photo lab.

I wanted to ask, *"Mommy, why are you and Uncle Rusty burning up money?"* But instead, I silently backed away and returned to the house. They were so focused on their task that my presence went unnoticed. I knew, of course, that money was meant for purposes other than burning, but even at this early stage in my life, little that Mommy did surprised me.

Those incinerated dead presidents would hold their mystery for nearly half a century before I finally put all, or almost all, the pieces together. It was kind of like finishing a thousand-piece jigsaw and finding that one piece is still missing, forever lost.

***

Decades later, as I was going through some old trunks the angels wouldn't let Mother haul with her through the pearly gates, a faded newspaper clipping, a scrap really, returned me to that garage when I'd been five or six and had gone out to investigate the burning smell.

About the same time as the money barbecue was heating up in our garage, a brief article had appeared in the Reno, Nevada, newspaper. The title announced: *Sparks Man Arrested "Holding the Bag" Full of Counterfeit. Denies Guilt; Trial Slated.*

"*Wesley Cisco Richards, formerly connected with the Owl Bar in Sparks, who was recently arrested in a Fallon house of ill fame in possession of a bag full of counterfeit money, yesterday pleaded innocent in federal court in Carson City. Mr. Richards is formally charged with possession of counterfeit money. He is alleged to have been trying to persuade one of the owners of the Fallon Institution to finance him in going into wholesale production of the phony money. He was represented yesterday by Attorney Frank Peterson, and Stan Brown was in charge of the prosecution on behalf of the U.S. District Attorney's Office.*"

The Wesley Cisco Richards cited in the newspaper article was my mother's middle brother, the man we came to know as "Uncle Cisco." Women, men, and money have always been the necessary ingredients for the world's oldest profession, but it seems that Uncle Cisco was introducing a new twist. He had gone to a "house of ill fame," located a few miles outside of Reno, not to sample the madam's wares, but to persuade her to help him peddle his.

While the Jacksons were roasting in our garage, Uncle Cisco had been sitting in the Washoe County Jail, hoping for bail. It is my understanding that he used his free phone call to alert some family member that there was additional "product" curing on clothes lines strung throughout his apartment like so much wash hanging out to dry. Someone, possibly Uncle Rusty, had made a quick trip to the Reno area and returned with it to our garage for the cremation ceremony I had stumbled upon.

But part of the mystery remains to this day, that missing puzzle piece. The money-burning sink in the garage was right next to the darkroom (photo lab) that Dad had built for my photographer mother. What I never learned was the full extent of how much she helped in Uncle Cisco's money-making scheme?

MEETING GOD

The "money mystery" was only the first of the many "mysteries" I'd discover in my life. And the next one was the "biggie."

I first heard God speak when I was just six years old. It was Christmas Eve, and Mother had taken me to midnight Mass. It was the first time I remember being in a church.

When we entered, the church was dark, dimly lit by the candles flickering at the shrines of the saints. We slipped into a pew about four rows back from the altar rail. As more worshippers arrived, I kept getting pushed along the hard wooden pew, polished smooth by the backsides of conger-gants. As I leaned back my feet dangled, not quite touching the extended kneeler. It too, was a plain, hard, wood, unlike the cushy pews and kneelers that would grace the mausoleum-like structure that would replace our almost cozy church a few years later.

At exactly midnight, the semi-darkness exploded into bril-liant white as what seemed like a million lights burst on all at once. The pew seemed to shake as "Angels We Have Heard on High" thundered from above and behind me as if it were the angels themselves welcoming the baby Jesus. Just as I turned to look back towards the source of the singing, half expecting to see multi-winged seraphim, or at least chubby cherubim, the priest processed by our pew in his gold and white vestments. As he passed, the air was filled with a new odor: incense, *how God smelled.*

The church was packed, and about the only thing I could see for most of the service was people's backsides. Except when they knelt down. Then, I could stand on the kneeler and just see the priest's head and part of his gold vestment. And that's when I heard him talking with God. They spoke in a strange language that only he and God could understand. The priest would say something, and then God would reply; in multiple voices, as if the entire Trinity were there conversing with Fr. Murphy, just a few feet from where I stood on tiptoes on that rickety kneeler, clinging to the back of the pew in front of me.

And that's how I became a part of "Catholicworld." Not only was the church God's house, but He was there and would talk to you, right out loud, at least if you were a priest. A priest—suddenly a very impressive person to be.

In 1955 I only knew about three kinds of people: Catholics, Protestants, and the godless Communists in a place called Russia. There were only two things I needed to know about the Russians. One, we prayed for their conversion every Sunday at Mass, and two: they were going to blow us all up with the atom bomb. The first of these things I learned in Church, and the other I learned from the television set in my aunt's living room. My family didn't own a TV, so I'd sit on the floor and glue myself to the tube when we visited my dad's sister every few weeks. We often got to her house just about the time the news started. A solemn-faced man would intone the dangers of Communism and its horrible leader with his finger on a button that could blast us all to smithereens. This was often accompanied by a demonstration of how the demon bomb worked. One little ball, like you used to play jacks, would bump into two more, which would hit two more, and then four, until they were bouncing all over the thirteen-inch black and white screen, visual evidence that Russia was just a day or two away from blowing up our whole country. I didn't exactly understand how rubber balls could blow me up, but neither did I understand how the man could be inside the television. Yet there he was.

I know that later I must have practiced bomb drills in grade school; following the Sisters' orders to slide under our desks, stick our head between our knees, and pray. I have blocked those memories out. I already knew what I needed to know. It was from that little television screen that I learned what fear was.

The other group, the Protestants, were even more dangerous. All the Russians could do was kill me, but the Protestants could cause me to lose my immortal soul, and spend eternity shoveling coal for the devil. We could pray for the Russians, because, probably, they didn't know any better. But the Protestants—they knew. As the Sisters were to tell us, they had once been part of the one, true, church—the Catholic One—but they had revolted, and rejected, not Jesus perhaps but the pope in Rome; and that seemed to be what really mattered.

It was hard to tell exactly who a Protestant was as they looked the same as everybody else. About the only way you could know for sure, unless someone told you, was on Sunday, when they went to a different church than I did. I went to "public" school for first grade, and I knew that some of my classmates were Protestant. But you couldn't tell by looking.

And, as far as I could tell, being Protestant was their only fault. They didn't go around kicking dogs or kidnapping children. And I couldn't figure out how they got to be Protestants in the first place. I was told that they lacked the "grace" to believe in the one true faith. Grace—that was a tough one. I knew it was real because all my religion teachers told me so. It was grace, given to us by God to help us believe in Him and be Catholic. I never really understood it, but I believed in it. I had to because otherwise, I might become a Protestant, or worse, if there was anything.

Well, enough about Protestants. By the middle of the last century, the American Catholic Church had almost come of age. The bishops had decreed at the Council of Baltimore in 1874 that the parish priest was to build a Catholic school, even before he constructed a church to house Jesus in the tabernacle. It worked. Several Catholic school generations later those hordes of unwashed European immigrants had learned English. "No Irish Need Apply" signs had vanished, and Catholic politicians were running many of the cities where those immigrants had settled, supported by Billy-club-toting Irish policemen. Five years later the immigration would be complete when Joe Kennedy got his son elected president, probably the greatest event in American Catholicism since Jesus's resurrection.

Why all of this matters, is because of what would happen to the church itself, and how that would affect me a few years later when I became a teenager.

Now I didn't have all this figured out that first night in church, but it was the beginning.

My timing with finding God was good. I had just stopped believing in Santa Claus a couple of nights before that midnight Mass. As he did every year, Santa came to visit us, not down our non-existent chimney, and not on Christmas Eve, but through the front door a couple of nights early. But this year, I noticed that when Santa came, Uncle Rusty wasn't in the room with us. And then there were Santa's shoes. They looked an awful lot like Uncle Rusty's. I studied Santa more carefully as he spoke to each of my younger brothers, noticing a small tear in his red pants. After Santa had gone, and Uncle Rusty returned from an errand, his pants exactly matched the color I saw through the tear in Santa's.

I was taken aback, but my discovery didn't provide any great trauma, and I didn't share my new knowledge with anybody: my parents, Uncle Rusty, or my three (younger) brothers. By the time Christmas came around the following year, I was in Catholic school, and Santa had been replaced by Jesus. I knelt before the statue of the Sacred Heart of Jesus in that same church and prayed: *"Dear Jesus. Happy Birthday. I'm glad you made it so that we get the gifts on your birthday. I just want one thing this year: a white horse, like Silver, the Lone Ranger's horse. Thank you, Jesus."*

I guess Jesus was out of horses that year because no horse of any color showed up under the tree. He would come close, though, with the pony a few years later. It was a bit disappointing; but then, Santa hadn't always answered my requests either. But maybe Jesus wasn't out of horses. Maybe it was something else. Maybe the only person whose prayers got answered was the one who could speak God's language: the priest. I'd sit on this one for a few years yet.

But first—the circus.

THE SWORD SWALLOWER

"Boys and girls, do *not* try this at home!" As he warned us, the sword swallower turned sideways on the small, raised stage to give the audience a better view. The sword flashed a rainbow of colors back at the lights in the top of the tent as he raised it to his parted lips. We watched, four young brothers, as it slid slowly past his Adam's apple. "Do you think it's gonna come out his bottom?" asked my youngest brother, the one we called TT.

"I don't think it's long enough," I said. "But be quiet. Don't talk so loud."

As the handle guard touched his lips, the sword swallower released the blade. He opened his arms wide and faced the audience showing that his feat was skill, not trickery. As some applauded and others felt queasy, he reversed his act and withdrew the sword bloodlessly.

Technically, it wasn't home, but the next morning found us in a hotel dining room waiting for our breakfast. Uncle Rusty leaned over to Mother and said, in a voice so calm he could have announced the Second Coming of Christ like he was telling a bedtime story, "Mac, I think one of your boys is trying to swallow his knife." Sure enough, my middle brother—the one Dad nicknamed Bull because he claimed he looked like a baby bull moose when Mother brought him home from the hospital—had a butter knife about halfway down his four-year-old throat and was starting to gag. Instead of screaming, Mother reached over and held Bull's chubby fingers in hers while Rusty went around the table and helped her extract the knife without further damage, except possibly to Bull's pride. The customers at the adjoining tables who saw what was happening gasped. They muttered about how lucky that little boy was. What was luckier, for them anyway, was that Bull had decided to imitate the sideshow's sword swallower and not its knife thrower. That guy tossed daggers while blindfolded at a woman spinning on a giant wooden wheel twenty feet in front of him.

There was no blood on the knife pulled from my brother's throat. The only red substance on any of the knives at breakfast that morning was strawberry jam. But had it been blood, it would have been "circus" blood—and not just "circus" blood, but "circus owner" blood.

At the time of the knife swallowing attempt, we had been traveling with the circus for several weeks. In some ways, we liked the sideshow better than the circus performance itself and watched it every time Mother would let us. It was what they called a Ten-in-One, referring to the number of acts and the huge banners that were attached to the outside of the sideshow tent, promising marvels that even God couldn't make happen. But it did have some weird stuff. Besides the sword swallower and knife thrower, there was the guy who could juggle and then eat fire and another man, the "Human Pincushion," who stuck knitting needles clear through his arms and cheeks. None of us ever tried to imitate him.

"Boys," my mother had said to her then brood of four sons the week that I, the oldest had finished first grade, "I'm taking you to your first circus. You'll love it. You're going to see elephants and lions and tigers, trapeze artists like your mommy was when she was little, and clowns, like my Uncle Savoy." The circus in question was not coming to our hometown. It was in Wisconsin, over two thousand miles away; and, according to the newspaper article Mother had published in our local paper upon our return, the trip took some two months in the summer of 1956.

"Ring Bros. Circus" was owned by my mother's older brother Franco. It was called "Ring Bros." to intentionally confuse it with the much larger and more famous "Ringling Brothers." I suppose that my uncle thought he could avoid lawsuits because my grandfather had named his last son after John Ringling, of the more famous circus family. So, the show's official name was Ring(ling)'s Brother's Circus, a circus owned by Ringling's brother, a true fact. That brother, Ringling, whom we knew as Uncle Rusty for his red hair, was joining us on our trek.

Our "wheels" were what Mother referred to as her "Hail Mary" car. It was a 1952 Willy's Jeep wagon: a two-toned green, stick shift on the column, and windows all around. It had two doors plus a tailgate; the top part of which opened upwards and served as our air conditioning.

Per my mother's specs, it was a custom job; Dad had done the customizing. He took out all but the front bench seat, leaving the interior bare steel except for the cloth headliner. Then he installed two-by-two-inch wooden rails along the sides, just below the windows. A hinged plywood platform fit atop the rails, filling the vehicle from the back of the driver's seat to the tailgate. This served as seating for us kids, a viewing platform, and a bed for campouts—or a two-thousand-mile trip to go see the circus. It had plenty of room for sightseeing, coloring, playing with our plastic army men, and the more than occasional fight. Seatbelts were a thing of the future.

The Jeep was also beneficial for going to the drive-in movies. We would go, already dressed in our "jammies," prepared to fall asleep during the second feature, after the intermission and cartoons. An added benefit was that all but one kid was usually stuffed under the platform until after we passed the ticket booth, thereby reducing the cost of admission.

The other major addition was the "grub box" that Dad had built, which fit under the bed, just inside the tailgate. Also made of sturdy plywood, its slanted front opened to provide a food prep surface and to reveal sections containing a Coleman stove, metal dishes, and a variety of staples useful on a camping/fishing trip. A fair bit of the food provisions were often "C rations," the forerunner of today's military MREs (Meals Ready to Eat).

Dad was a supply sergeant for the California National Guard, and each year he would return from his annual three-week guard training exercises with his car stuffed with boxes of the "C rations." After removing the three-pack of "smoke 'em if you got 'em" cigarettes in each box, he would let us kids take the crackers, cookies, and round cake of chocolatey something. The rest—the round army-green cans which contained desperation foods like over-cooked spaghetti, beanies and weenies, SOS for the hard tack biscuits, and something distantly related to hamburger—was put in the grub box.

Mother was aware that motor vehicles required gas, oil, and water to function, but preventive maintenance, especially brakes and tires, escaped her notice. As the car put on a few years and miles, this oversight became more of a factor in getting from point A to point B.

The bane of the car's existence was Rindler Hill, a particularly steep incline that God had absentmindedly placed between our home in Fairfield and the Bay Area, some thirty-five miles to the southwest. That is where some of the highlights of modern civilization were located, such as Mother's over-used OB/GYN, the Capwell's department store, and See's Candy. With today's freeway and a newer vehicle, you might not even notice it, but in the Jeep on old Highway 40, it was a different story.

For those unfamiliar with Catholic practices, the "Hail Mary" was originally a prayer, not a football pass. "Okay," Mother would say, "We're coming up on Rindler Hill. Start praying." We prayed "Hail Mary, full of grace, the Lord is with thee..." to protect us from brake failure going down Rindler Hill and "Holy Mary, Mother of God, pray for us sinners..." to help the engine and transmission trying to make the climb back up. It must have worked because I don't remember us breaking down or dying in an accident.

We got ready for our circus trip by packing the Jeep. Our clothing trousseau included the matching pinstriped train engineer suits we often all wore because I had once told my mother that I wanted to change my name to "Engineer." Also tucked in there were "Wyatt Earp" outfits of cowboy shirts, hats, and bolo ties—which was our current fascination—and custom-made white jackets with an elephant and "Ring Bros. Circus" emblazoned on the back in red, silver, and blue glitter. The space under the bed offered plenty of room for all our bedding, belongings, and the treasures still to be collected, such as Mexican sombreros and the live "horned toads" we caught in Texas on the way home. A necessary final touch was the empty quart Coke bottle, which served as a makeshift urinal between gas stations. This accommodated several small boys—not at the same time—and could even be emptied in transit, although it evoked fewer complaints if the disposer remembered to close the back windows first.

And off we went. I'm sure we had planned for an early departure, but in keeping with Mother's lifelong practice of training to be late for her own funeral, it was well into the afternoon before the Jeep rumbled to life. The first stop was Reno, where we filled the Jeep with gas; got something to eat; dropped a few nickels; and emptied the Coke bottle. Night was falling as we left the lights of the "Biggest Little City in the

World" behind. Sometime, after us kids had fallen asleep, we pulled over for the night, just by the side of the highway, near an overhang of some sort. I don't know how long I had been sleeping when I heard my uncle's whispered shout to Mother, "Mac, I hear something!" By the time he had opened the passenger door and jumped out, I was fully awake. He returned seconds later. "I think a landslide is starting. We need to go!" His last words were still forming when Mother jammed the car into gear and floored the gas pedal. I don't know if any mountain fell that night. I just know we weren't under it.

As the Hail Mary car wheezed up the Rockies and crossed the Great Divide, Mother told us about her own childhood and life on her parent's circus, a pre-curser of the one we were on our way to see.

"My Daddy..." she began. She always called him My Daddy, as if she were canonizing a saint. "He owned his own circus when I was born. My Daddy's show didn't travel by train like Ringling Brother's or some of the other big circuses, but we didn't go by horse and wagon either. My Daddy's circus went from town to town by truck. He claimed it was the first motorized circus in America. We moved to a new town every day, but My Daddy never showed on a Sunday, out of respect for it being the Lord's Day. And My Daddy didn't cuss, and he never allowed other men to cuss around the ladies." She then went on to tell a long story about how he may have killed a man who insulted his wife, my grandmother. In order to escape the county sheriff, he dressed himself as a woman and fled, rejoining the circus several weeks and a couple of states later.

"When I was a little boy..." Mother would often begin. She frequently referred to herself as a little boy in her stories. I don't know if this is so we, all boys, could relate, or for dramatic effect, or because of her own view of the fate of little girls, that is, she herself, as she was growing up. Some things were unsaid, some stories untold, and it would not surprise me if she had been abused at the hands of her uncle, her dad's younger brother and erstwhile partner. Her "Uncle Cisco," a completely different character than her money-printing brother, was a true villain, whose name she always hissed through clinched teeth, regardless of context. He played the devil to her daddy's good angel.

"When I was a little boy, I performed in the circus. I think I started when I was about four. I was a contortionist and could twist my body in all kinds of ways. I also did the 'rolling globe' act. My uncle Savoy would help me get up on a giant wooden ball, bigger than I was, and I would roll it up a wide board with my feet. When I got to the top, the whole tent would cheer for me."

"Weren't you afraid, Mommy?" one of us asked her from the back of the Jeep.

"Not of that," she said. "The scary part was something I barely remember." And that's when she first told us about the Iron Jaw and the baby's fall.

"In the winter, the off-season, we lived at the Ranch. My Daddy owned five hundred acres on the Medina River in Pipe Creek. My brother Franco and I each had our own pony. Mine was named 'Teddy,' and he loved me and was really sweet, except if he got tired of you riding him, he would go under a tree branch and knock you off. Franco's pony was 'Captain,' and he was mean and liked to bite people. My Daddy paid five hundred silver dollars to the man to buy me my pony. We had to watch out for rattlesnakes cuz they were all over. We had a spring on the river by our house and a bunch of us kids would go swimming there a lot. Sometimes we'd also take our elephant with us. She was named 'Maxine,' same as me."

Swimming with elephants? Our own Mommy? When she was littler than we were?

This should have surprised us, but I guess when your mother tells you that she was a boy when she was little, not much else can.

Mother was a good storyteller, and some of her tales were

a bit tall, but most were in the "truth is stranger than fiction" category, and she filled the miles of highway and kept back seat fighting to a minimum.

"Mommy, I need to wee-wee," one of my brothers interrupted her.

"Can you wait a little? It's just a few miles to the next gas station."

"No, Mommy, I can't. I gotta go real bad, right now."

"Well then, just use the Coke bottle."

"It's too full."

"Rusty, can you empty the Coke bottle?"

"Okay, Mac."

My uncle Rusty, riding shotgun, rolled down the passenger side window, took the nearly full bottle, and let the contents flow out onto the highway.

Mother was I would call a "reluctant prude." Profanity of any sort was absolutely forbidden because that's the way "My Daddy" raised her.

If us kids needed to eliminate liquid waste from our growing bodies, we had to use the word "wee-wee." No other word or combination of words was acceptable. We couldn't pee, take a piss, go number one, or even urinate. Number two, a.k.a. defecate, take a dump, shit, or crap, were to be expressed only as "doo-doo." My mother's best friend and my godmother, Dorothy, who could give most of the saints a run for their money, would occasionally slip up. She'd say, "Excuse me, Mac, I need to go tinkle," which would immediately be met with a *"Dorothy!* It's wee-wee!" as though my godmother had called God a Communist or something.

The male protuberance that was required to transfer the wee-wee from the human body to another location was known, and only known—no other description was acceptable—as a boy's "wee-wee stick."

Marriage forced Mother to make a couple of exceptions. "Damn" and "Hell" were not considered cursing, as they were an integral part of Dad's vocabulary, and even Mother didn't tell Dad how to live his life, especially in serious matters such as cussing.

When we got into the Great Plains, Mother switched gears. "If you boys are going to spend time on the circus, you need to learn how to talk like circus people talk, and I'm going to teach you. It's called 'Carnie,' and once you learn, only the circus people will know what you are saying. The 'townies' or 'Rubes' won't be able to understand you."

"Ciazarn" or "Carnie" is a type of pig Latin used mostly in the past by circus and carnie employees as their private language. It inserts an "iz" into words or syllables, usually after the first consonant unless the word begins with a vowel. It sounds, and is, simple, but when spoken rapidly, it's indecipherable to the untrained ear.

"Let's say you want to say *mommy*," she began. "In Carnie, it's 'm-iz-ommy.' Or your name, Engineer. That would be 'Iz-En-giz-in-iz-eer,' or your uncle Rusty's name; that's Iz-uncle Rizusty. Okay. Now let's try a whole sentence: 'We are going to the circus to see the elephants.' That's: 'W-iz-e iz-are giz-oing t-iz-u thiz-e ciz-ur-ciz-us t-iz-u siz-ee thiz-e izel-ize-phiz-ants.' You try it."

We learned Carnie while the Hail Mary car conquered Iowa and Nebraska. It's not too complicated, and we were young. But spoken quickly, it does confuse an unfamiliar listener, which is the purpose. The first sentence Mother taught us would sound like this to the untrained ear, "Wizeizaregizoingtizuthizecizurcizustizusizeethizeizelizephizants."

I was beginning to understand the secret language of the circus with its ability to include those who were "with it" and exclude outsiders. Maybe that's how God's secret language worked too.

CIRCUS BOY

We arrived in "Cheesehead" country about a week after leaving home, where we got our first view of the circus and met my Uncle Franco. Even in elevator shoes, he was a "big man" in a small body, not much over five feet. His several marriages were always to women at least six inches taller than he was. He could easily have passed for one of the car salesmen who sold him his annual Cadillac automobile, a status symbol, along with his circus and assorted wives and girlfriends. These trappings were necessary for him to fill the shoes of the original Franco, my grandfather, always known on his own circus as "Boss" Richards. Somewhat like "W" of Iraq War fame, my uncle's goal seems to have been to show that he was a bigger and better man than Dear Old Dad.

Uncle Franco showed us around the lot, stopping at the concession wagon to give us some popcorn in a purple cellophane cone, which held considerably less of the treat than it appeared. "Y'all want some popcorn? Hey, Babe, get these fellas some popcorn," he said to the young woman in the trailer. "They're my nephews from California. Mac, you want any?" We also got a cup of "flukum" to wash down the salty popcorn—more salt equals more beverages sold. "Flukum" was the slang name for the inexpensive soft drink of questionable origin sold by circuses at the time.

"Uncle Franco," I asked, "is this whole circus yours?"

"She sure is, son. Tents, trucks, animals, all of it."

"Can we pet the elephants?" my brother Von interrupted.

"I reckon. We'll go over to the menagerie in a bit, after the crowd clears out. I don't usually let people touch my elephants But, ya'll are family. You boys know your momma was named after an elephant? She was. Maxine, the elephant on my dad's show. I got a little elephant, named her after my other sister, your Aunt Bonnie. She was so little when we got her that my wife Lucy had to feed her from a bottle."

"And the lions, can we pet the lions too?" asked another brother.

"No, you can't pet the lions. Damn, Mac, your kids sure ask a lot of questions."

"They're boys, Franco," Mother replied, "and this is their first circus."

As we passed the little souvenir stand, we all stopped and gawked. In a generous move—for him—he let us select a toy at the souvenir stand. I remember kewpie dolls and intriguing little paper birds which "sang" as you twirled them around on a string attached to a reed stick.

But when it came time to choose, we all said, "I want one of those whips," the ones like the lion tamer used.

A couple of days later, Uncle Franco even unrolled the wad of hundreds, which he always carried with him and peeled off an entire twenty-dollar bill. "Here, Mac. Go buy your kids some cap guns to match their cowboy outfits." Even at six, I remember the not-quite curse words, her response to his "generosity." After all, this was the older brother who had taken most of his parent's insurance money to start his first circus, leaving his sister, my mother, with nothing except their younger siblings to raise by herself, at only sixteen, after both their parents had died of the Great Depression.

Speaking of uncles, it turns out that part of the reason for taking our trek to the circus was to help my younger uncle, Rusty, lick his wounds. He was only two years old when his parents died, so my mother was essentially his mother, as well. Unlike his older brother, he was a good and kind man. Unlike his older brother, who supposedly shot himself in the foot to avoid military service, he'd served his country during the Korean conflict. He was stationed at some extremely sensitive post in the Aleutian Islands, where he carried a cyanide capsule in his pocket to be taken should he ever be captured. While he was defending his country at the edge of the world, his high school sweetheart Beverly waited for him. Well, almost. Just before his service was up, he got a "Dear John" letter from her, ending their engagement. To help him drown his sorrows his sister/mother took us all on a trip to the circus.

Mother hadn't lied. In the weeks we traveled with the show, we got to see lions, tigers, and elephants as well as ponies, emus, and giant snakes. We got to see the circus performances nearly every day. Unlike his Dad, Uncle Franco had no hesitation showing on Sundays. In fact, it was the best day because it allowed for an extra matinee.

***

When we first walked into the Big Top to take our seats on the backless bleachers (because Uncle Franco had only given us general admission tickets), the tent was alive with activity. People were already sitting down while the "butchers" were making their first runs through the bleachers yelling, "popcorn, peanuts, snow cones." "Roughnecks"—the men who did the menial work on the show—were clanging together the cages of the big cat act, which kicked off the performance after the opening "spec" parade. Others were re-checking the rigging for the trapeze act. Across the tent, the band was warming up. So many smells were mixing together—sugary cotton candy, newly laid sawdust, animal dung, and human sweat—that my nose just gave up trying to sort it all out, joining my eyes and ears. If anything could be more exciting, it was hard to imagine.

The performance began with the entire company of fully costumed performers and animals making several turns around the hippodrome. This was known as the opening "spec," or spectacle: a feature of nearly every circus.

The first act was the lions and tigers performing in a large cage in the center ring. The animals raced through a "cage tunnel" from their homes in one of the trucks to the cage the roughnecks had just assembled. The lion tamer was dressed in a tan jumpsuit with a holstered pistol strapped around his waist. He wore a white pith helmet and carried a whip, a real one, curled in his right hand. As the animals rushed in, amid screams and yells from the crowd, he'd crack his whip, and occasionally fire blanks in the air from his pistol. Each lion or tiger had his own pedestal to sit on. Sometimes, one creature would seem to get in the wrong place, and another would growl at it and force it to move. I never found out if they were trained to do this or just got confused. For the next few minutes, the animals would leap through hoops and over one another, snarling and growling. One of them was trained to walk on his hind legs, towering over the tamer, as if they were dancing. At the conclusion of the act, an assistant would hand the lion tamer a special hoop which he would then set afire. After some coaxing, the largest of the tigers would jump through the flaming hoop to the roars of the crowd. It probably took that tiger more "faith" to jump through that flaming hoop than for me to believe that Fr. Murphy could talk to God or that he could change bread into Jesus's body.

The first of the clown acts came on as the animals returned to their cages on the trucks and the roughnecks took the performance cage apart and stacked the panels off to the side. The clown act I remember the best was the one that had two clowns run in on a little fire engine pretending to put out fires. They kept throwing buckets of water, which ended up on one another instead of the fire. Finally, one of the clowns pretended to be on fire herself, and the other chased her around the tent with a bucket finally throwing it past the clown and towards the crowd. As the front couple of rows of people ducked and shrieked, they were drenched not with water but with confetti.

"Look up, boys, to the top of the tent," Mother pointed toward a figure in leotards and sequins. "That's your Aunt Lucy, Uncle Franco's wife. The other trapeze artist is her sister, Gail."

We looked up, mesmerized, as the two women seemed to fly like they had wings. They would twist and turn, exchanging places on the trapeze bar.

"That's like what my mother and I used to do in my Daddy's circus, as she reminded us about the Iron Jaw act."

Uncle Rusty was sitting with us that first day we watched the circus. His jaw was anything but iron as it dropped. Like us, he was mesmerized, but not with the performance. He never even saw Aunt Lucy, only her little sister Gail.

Another clown act followed, this one featuring dogs. Different breeds of dogs, always with tails wagging, jumped through hoops and over one another, yipping all the while. The biggest laughs came for the large dog, who pushed a smaller dog around in a baby carriage. The big dog wore a granny dress and a bonnet, and the little dog wore a diaper and held a baby bottle.

The first part of the performance closed with a tightrope walker. She'd begin by climbing up an inclined section of wire until she reached a small platform from which she set out on the tight rope stretched across the center ring. She started very tentatively as if she were about to fall off and then her tricks got progressively more challenging. She'd walk forwards, backwards, and skip rope while balancing on the wire. At the end, she was standing on only one foot and twirling large plastic neon rings on her other foot and both arms.

Halfway through the performance there was an intermission, which ushered in my own lifelong participation in the family circus tradition. It was during the intermission of the performances of this first circus, that I was introduced to cotton candy and circus balloons.

Other acts followed, although I can't remember the exact order. One of the jugglers would twirl plates. He'd set a plate spinning at the end of a dowel rod and then balance it on his forehead or chin. Seemed like he always dropped one at each performance. It shattered as it hit the ground. At the climax of his performance, he had half a dozen plates spinning, balanced on several parts of his body.

When another clown came into the ring, he was wearing a hobo hat and carrying an umbrella, except that the umbrella had no fabric covering its spokes. This clown climbed up on a little stand and tried to walk on a rope strung between two such stands. He hardly needed a net as the rope was just a couple of feet off the ground. As he stood on the rope, it gyrated, threatening to toss him to the ground. Always looking like he was about to fall off, he managed to walk back and forth between the two stands, balancing himself with that broken umbrella.

"That's just like my Uncle Savoy," Mother whispered. "He was a clown, and he did 'slack wire.' That's slack wire, that rope—it's really wire—that he's walking on. Because it sways, it's a lot more difficult than the tightrope walkers, although it's not as dangerous because it's low to the ground."

Four beautiful white horses ran out into the ring. A man cracking a long whip led them through various tricks, but I was much more intrigued by the figure standing, not sitting, atop the first horse's back; a beautiful young woman whose blonde hair flowed behind her as she stood on her horse in a white singlet, trimmed in gold. I was immediately in love, but the girl was probably twice my age, so my love went unrequited.

Almost last, but certainly not least, was the elephant performance. The big beasts would parade and walk across an impossibly small beam between two metal tubs, a pachyderm version of tightrope. They would also stand nearly upright on their hind legs and they ended the act by kneeling on all fours, almost, but not quite, crushing the prone female performer lying beneath them; before picking her up in their trunk and carrying her out of the tent.

The finale of the show was the Human Cannonball. All eyes turned to a monstrous silver truck that would make a Hummer tuck its tail between its legs. It entered the tent ever so slowly and made a complete circuit around the hippodrome. It turned, backed up, moved forward, seeking just the right position as the band played a track from an Alfred Hitchcock movie.

The truck was a rolling platform for a giant cannon, its barrel nearly two feet in diameter. As the band played, the cannon raised itself from the truck bed until it was pointed at the other end of the big top. A man in a silver suit, dwarfed by the truck and its cannon, climbed up the outside of the elevated barrel, his arms outstretched for balance. At the tip of the barrel, he hesitated for a moment or so before waving to the crowd, as though it was his final gesture. Then he disappeared inside.

Now the band really got going, as the ringmaster primed the crowd about the danger of the stunt and cautioned them to silence. All eyes were on the end of the canon or the net everyone just noticed at the other end of the tent, nearly a hundred feet away. The loud BANG shook the seats and, as smoke flashed, a silvery figure, a human bullet, was hurled from the barrel through the air.

***

There was a lot more to the circus than performances. Watching the tent being put up was its own entertainment. The "roughnecks" would unroll the massive canvas onto the ground. Then what seemed like hundreds of long metal stakes were driven into the ground around the edges. Next the center poles were raised, often with the help of Suzie the elephant. The canvas was attached to the center poles via "bale rings" and raised into the air, and "wah-lah," it started to look like a circus tent. Before the most important part, the sidewalls, which blocked the view and forced people to pay admission, were added, trucks carrying the lumber for the seating drove in. The seating was unloaded and assembled: flat red benches six or seven tiers high for general admission, and the blue section of folding chairs, at ground level just in front of the performance rings, which cost fifty cents extra.

The show also had a menagerie tent, for a separate charge. I remember a zebra, the first I had seen, some caged apes, the lions, also caged, and the elephants staked and chained, their trunks swinging back and forth along the ground, grabbing tufts of hay, or picking up dirt to give themselves a dust bath. At the other end of the tent were many of the more domestic animals, such as the performing horses. Sawdust was under my feet, and even if I covered my ears against the shrieks, growls, and whinnies, and closed my eyes, the smell of rotting fruit mixed with the aromas of various animal dung reminded me where I was.

My uncle's circus lacked a calliope like the one his father had owned. Instead, it featured a live band: a mini orchestra of seven or eight musicians. I think they were the first live musicians I had ever seen, not counting the church organist, and I never tired of listening to them, especially their flourishes when the top-hatted ringmaster announced the grand entry. Their music added suspense to the more danger-ous acts and cued us to laugh at the clowns' antics.

We took most of our meals in the "cook tent," where food was prepared several times a day, and the whole crew got fed. We sat at portable wooden tables covered with red-checked oilcloth and assembled in a manner like the bleachers.

I had never seen "white butter."

"Why is the butter white?" I asked of no one in particular.

"That's not butter. It's margarine," no one in particular answered. "This is Wisconsin, the nation's foremost dairy state. They make lots of real butter here and don't like people using margarine, so they made a law prohibiting adding color to the white margarine so it couldn't be confused with the real thing."

We sat on the managers' and performers' side of the din-ing tent where the people, like the margarine, were all white. The roughnecks, or regular workers, sat on their own side.

While we were visiting the circus, one of the performers "adopted" us. It was a young woman in her early teen years, the same one who enthralled me atop the white horse. The photo I have of her shows her standing in her sequined white singlet with one of the elephants. She and Mother became fast friends. I think she must have reminded Mother of herself when she was a child performer on her own daddy's circus back in the twenties. I think the young woman, Sandy, was re-lated to my aunt Lucy, Uncle Franco's wife of the moment.

Sandy could stand on a horse's bare back while it raced around the center ring. She wasn't afraid to let an elephant pick her up in its trunk and ride atop the beast's head. And she was beginning to learn some of the basic trapeze tricks. But she couldn't drive a car.

Mother fixed that. In the afternoons she would place her four sons in the back of the Hail Mary car, on our bed/view/fighting board while she'd sit on the bench seat next to Sandy, who was behind the wheel.

The "classroom" portion of Mother's driver training course went like this: "The pedal nearest your right foot is the gas," she explained. "Next to that is the brake. You operate both of those with your right foot—not at the same time, of course. The other pedal is the clutch. You push it down with your left foot when you want to change gears. You already know what the steering wheel is and what it does. That white knob just to the right of the steering wheel, that's the gear shift, so you can go slow, medium, or fast. You move it in an 'H' pattern to change gears. Straight down is low. Up and out is second. Down and out is high. And, if you want to go backwards, reverse, pull it towards you and go straight up. Right in the middle is neutral. In neutral, the car sits still."

She looked up to make sure the girl was still paying attention. "Now, let's give 'er a try," she encouraged. "Put the car in neutral. Don't forget to push in the clutch so you don't strip the gears. Now, turn on the key. By your left foot is a little button. When you step on it, the car's engine will start. Good. Now, give it a little gas, push in the clutch, and shift the gear into low."

The car lurched forward—and died.

"Whoa, Show Pony. You have to let the clutch out real slow. That's the trick. Let's try it again."

This time the Jeep jumped forward but kept going. In the back, we banged our heads on the headliner and scrunched down. The Jeep bounced through the rutted field.

After about twenty more minutes of practice, Mother said, "Great first day. Maybe by tomorrow or the next day, we can get you out on the road."

Within a week, Sandy was driving—maybe not one of the circus semis yet, but good enough to get by.

One day, as Sandy, Mother, and us four boys were walking away from the cook tent, Sandy pointed out one of the roughnecks to my mother and whispered, in "Ciazarn," the circus language we had learned during our travels. "Mizaxizine, kizeep, yizour kizids izawizay frizom thizat gizuy. Hize lizikes lizittle bizoys." I overheard her comment, and although I understood the Ciazarn words ("Maxine, keep your kids away from that guy. He likes little boys."), her meaning eluded me.

But her warning didn't escape Mother's notice and a few days later we left the circus and headed for home. I don't know if this was coincidence or because of Sandy's warning. I do know that in any "close calls" I would have in this area the potential abuser would be wearing a Roman collar, not a blue one.

We left without Uncle Rusty. His older brother had offered him a job, but it was his fascination with his sister-in-law Gail that sealed the deal.

My month on the circus changed me. I don't recall ever wanting to become a lion tamer, a trapeze artist or even a human bullet, but I did become a different person. After all, I had discovered my roots, where I had come from. I was a circus person. It was in my blood; I felt it down to my soul. This revelation was as significant as hearing God speaking in that little church a few months before.

The Catholic Church considers that baptism, one of its seven sacramental rituals, imparts a permanent mark on a person's soul. It's indelible. It can't be repeated, undone, or erased. For me, that mark was supposedly placed on my soul when I was baptized as an infant, but it didn't start to kick in until that Christmas Eve Mass when I had just turned six.

Knowing I was a circus person was like that. I was marked, and there was no way to undo it. You can't not be who you are. Even though I never wanted to be a performer, never sought center stage like my mother or grandmother had, there was still a desire, an urge, a drive—for travel, for adventure, for discovery. For having a different outlook on life than many of my fellows—and being okay with that. Maybe the experience got me ready for being different in another way; squirrelling myself away in a Catholic seminary, when my contemporaries were all doing what teenagers do.

The circus, not unlike God and His church and the priesthood, held a magical quality—women flying through the air seeming to defy gravity, men emerging unscathed from a cage of roaring beasts, people eating fire without fear. Although I saw all these things with my own eyes, I still couldn't quite believe I was seeing them.

With the church, it was the same, only backwards. A man talking with a God I could hear but not see. A piece of bread I could taste but not see the God/man it had become. I couldn't quite see these things with my own eyes, yet I was starting to believe them.

For most of my life, the priest and the circus in me would never be far apart.

SAVING PAGAN BABIES

"Gerald Meyers." Nobody moved. "Gerald Meyers!" Still, all the children and their parents sat in their brand-new plastic chairs, in the brand-new cafeteria, at the brand-new Holy Spirit School. "GERALD MEYERS," the principal, Sr. Mary Athanasius called a third time.

"Oh, that's you," my mother said as she pushed me toward the center of the room where they were assembling the second-grade class.

As soon as we had returned from our summer circus adventure my proud mother had dutifully followed all the instructions regarding my new uniform: salt and pepper corduroy pants, white short-sleeve shirt, and a blue pullover sweater from the approved Catholic School vendor, of course. Unfortunately, she also added a beanie, which only appeared on the girls' uniform list. Had I not noticed this fatal error the moment we walked into the cafeteria and shoved the offending article deep into her purse, I might not have lived through the first day of second grade. The girls needed the beanies to cover their heads whenever we went into the church—a demand of the sexist rules of 1950s Catholicism.

After a prayer and a blessing by the pastor, the principal had begun calling off the student names, a grade at a time.

"Gerald Meyers?"

"*That's not me,*" I thought. *"My name is 'Engineer.' Everybody knows that.*" Well, except for my school last year when they also got my name wrong. In first grade I had gone to Fairfield Elementary, the public school, because Holy Spirit, the Catholic one, was still being built. When I got to first grade wearing the little train engineer uniform Mommy always dressed me in, the name tag taped to my desk, written on lined paper, so I could learn to write it myself, spelled out N-o-v-e-d-u-a-n-e.

What was going on here? Was I a member of the name-a-year club? Why couldn't I just have one name like everybody else?

As best I could learn, here's the story. My dad was born in 1915 in Cat Spring, Texas, which is a place that could make a wide-spot-in-the-road think it was New York City. A country doctor had come from somewhere to help deliver the baby, a first son. After the family argued for what must have seemed like hours over who to name Dad after, the doctor announced that he was leaving. "Folks, I have to go now, so I am going to put down on the birth certificate the first four letters of the month in the name place and ya'll can have it changed when ya'll decide." It was November, and they never changed his name from Nove. I'm just glad he wasn't born in the spring.

When I came along, my parent's first child, and born in November to boot, there was no real choice. Well, almost none. My birth certificate, the one with the baby footprint on it and the gold seal, states a first name of Nove and a middle name of Duane.

But God needed a holy name, a saint. My godmother's first husband, who went down with his ship as all good captains are wont to do, rose from the briny to lend me his: Gerald. So, by the time I was three months old, and properly christened, my first name had become Noveduane with a middle name of Gerald, after the saint.

But that wasn't the end of it. I liked trains—big ones, real ones. One of my very first memories is of sitting with Dad in his 1950 Lincoln sedan at the train tracks a mile or so from our house on Evelyn Avenue in Albany. I was little, two or so, and it was also late at night, so maybe that's how he got me to settle down and go to sleep. He was in charge until Mommy got back from her job as a nightclub photographer.

We'd wait. Then we could hear the train coming. The railroad crossing gate would come down, right in front of our car and the lights would start flashing. The locomotive chugged by us pulling blocks of freight cars slowly through the industrial area as the ground shook like the San Francisco earthquake was starting again. It was a total experience, almost religious.

As the train rolled by, Dad would identify the various cars for me, the locomotive, the coal car, boxcars, flatcars, tankers, and the caboose.

I must have asked Dad, "What makes the train go?"

He probably said, "There's a man in the locomotive that drives the whole train. They call him the engineer."

Before I was three, I informed Mommy that I wanted to be a train driver, an engineer, and that I wanted to change my name to "Engineer."

She did it.

She started calling me "Engineer," and I have no memory of anyone calling me anything other than that, except my dad and his sister, until I started school. Mother herself used that name until her dying day.

But she didn't stop there. Along with my new name, she dressed me in pinstriped engineer overalls until I traded them in for a Catholic school uniform in the second grade. After serving as a miniature "engineer" through first grade, in a public school, no one was ever happier to put on a Catholic school uniform like all the other boys wore.

But evidently "Noveduane" was too much of a mouthful for the FOB (fresh off the boat) Irish nuns. Plus, it's always safer to use a saint's name, one they could be sure God would approve.

So now I was Gerald. But before my classmates started calling me "Jerry," the nuns learned to pronounce Noveduane and my classmates Nove. So for most of my life I've managed to have to answer to only Nove, or Engineer.

Until decades later, with 9/11. Until then I could probably buy an airplane ticket as Nove, or probably even Engineer. But since those terrorists crashed into New York, all my documents must be aligned like the stars and planets in an astrology reading. When traveling, I am once again the unpronounceable "Noveduane."

***

The Sisters of the Holy Faith came to our new Catholic school direct from the mothership in Ireland. Except for Sr. Mary Athanasius, the principal, who had been Americanized for a few years in the land of LaLa and Disney. I don't know exactly how they got to our school, but I know they didn't fly because their habits were anything but aerodynamic. These were no "flying nuns." Liftoff, except possibly during a tornado, was a physical impossibility, short of some kind of miracle.

Their black veils covered a white, U-shaped, three-sided box, which looked like stiff plastic but was likely heavily starched linen. The headgear appeared to entirely remove the nuns' peripheral vision. And yet, they somehow had eyes in the back of their heads, which could penetrate that black veil. Even the nicest of them (a relative term) could be writing on the chalkboard, back to the class, and spin in one smooth motion and fire the eraser at the head of a misbehaving student. Their accuracy would have made the young King David envious.

Fr. Murphy's thick brogue and God-like powers of persuasion could still only recruit four of them for the first year, so Holy Spirit opened with only four grades. The mothership promised another nun each year until we had a full crew.

Since Sr. Athanasius was busy with administrative and disciplinary duties, the first-grade teacher was "sister" Vera, one of the parish mothers with a teaching certificate. She taught all the kids in my family except me and outlasted all the original nuns and at least the first set of replacements.

My first teacher, in second grade, was the almost kindly Sr. Loyola. It was Sr. Loyola who introduced us to the Baltimore Catechism, the book with all the answers to all the questions the Church deemed worthy of being asked and prepared us for the biggest single moment in a Catholic child's life: First Holy Communion.

Sr. Mary of the Sacred Heart of Jesus, who was to become my third-grade teacher, was meaner than she was tall. Maybe she was trying to make up for being so short, or part of it was that she got stuck with such a cumbersome religious name. How would you like to have to answer to Sacred Heart all the time? She could take on even the gangliest boy and make him wish he'd listened the first time.

The last original nun taught fourth grade that first year. Her name was Sr. Perpetua, which I think means *forever*, but it didn't work out that way because she was the first of the nuns to leave. She was gone by the time I got to fourth grade, so I can't say much about her except that she was tall, had pale skin with lots of freckles, and could hike up her long black skirt to play a pretty good game of kickball during recess.

***

My own religious fervor first came to the attention of the Sisters of the Holy Faith during Christmas time of second grade. One of the good sisters' favorite organizations was the Holy Childhood Association, whose motto is *"Children helping children."* Our job was to save pagan babies, specifically their souls. You might think we could best do this by praying, but no. The deed was done by selling Christmas seals to our parents, neighbors, and relatives. The seals came in perforated pages of ten and little booklets of one hundred. The seals themselves, and the books they were in, showed a picture of the pagan babies, usually black, brown, or yellow children, looking at a white baby Jesus in his manger.

The sisters assured us that it was important work. If left alone, these children could die without baptism and couldn't get into heaven. As we all knew from our daily Baltimore Catechism lesson, *"God made us to know, love, and serve Him in this world and be happy with Him in the next (heaven)."* But: no baptism, no heaven. Fortunately, there were missionaries in these pagan lands anxious to baptize these little heathens. All they needed was some money. In the mid-1950s it cost one dollar, the price of a full booklet of Christmas seals, to get the job done. One book of stamps sold; one pagan baby saved for God.

You might be tempted to ask, *"If God made these little children in His likeness—*another catechism answer*—then why would He make it so hard for them to get to heaven?"* Good question. Not so good an answer.

It goes this way, more or less. Ever since St. Paul got knocked off his horse onto his ass (Acts 9:3–9), Christians have been seriously infected by the evangelization bug. "Come to Jesus; save your soul from eternal damnation; and maybe get eaten by a lion in the process." After the Roman emperor Constantine discovered that God and governance go well together, it was no longer dangerous to be Christian. It was even a requirement to get ahead.

Politics aside, the theological rationale for baptism was that we were all sinners and needed forgiveness. Jesus had already done the heavy lifting, so we just needed to turn our lives over to Him and get ourselves baptized.

But what about the babies, those seeming sinless innocents? Surely, they would not be banished to the eternal flame because their parents, if they even had any, omitted a little holy water? Saint Augustine blamed their sin on the apple: Eve's apple, "Here honey, try this. It's real tasty" (Genesis 3:6—not an exact translation). Because she persuaded Adam to take a bite, even the newly born are infected by this "original" sin. But should these poor babies wind up in hell? Not even St. Augustine was that cruel. Still, you can't have a heaven full of screaming unbaptized babies. He suggested that these "almost innocents" take up residence in a kind of heavenly waiting room called Limbo, which satisfied the Catholics, at least, for the next millennium and a half.

Hence the pagan babies' need for our services. Rather than risk these children having to wait in Limbo until the Judgment Day, we could get them baptized for the price of a few stickers.

So, right after Thanksgiving, each child in our school, Holy Spirit, was given a book of Christmas seals and expected to sell them to save a pagan baby. A simple calculation suggests the scope. Three or four hundred children per school and several thousand Catholic schools in the United States, and anyone can see that Jesus would have a very happy birthday indeed, if we all did our part. Not only that, but we got a little medal or scapular if we sold at least one book of stamps. This being America, there was a special prize for the child who sold the most stamps.

I took to the task with a vengeance. After I had exhausted the goodwill of my extended family, including the Baptist aunt I was forever trying to convert to the "true" faith, I sold Holy Childhood stickers to the newspaper lady who was my mother's boss, to customers coming out of Travis Market, our local grocery store, and to the neighbors for several blocks around. As might be expected, my best sale was to my saintly godmother, who bought an entire booklet of stamps.

I kept going back to Sr. Mary Loyola. "Sister, I need another book of stamps," I'd say as I handed her a dollar's worth of nickels and dimes. I sold a total of seven books, a school record, and felt as though I had single-handedly saved half the continent of Africa, like I was some kind of miniature missionary.

The most sacred place in our parish, the place that only the select few could lay eyes on, wasn't the tabernacle on the altar, but the inside of the nun's convent. The students at Holy Spirit School would watch the sisters come out the front door each morning and return after school in the afternoon. But none of us knew what happened within that cloister, letting our youthful imaginations run wild. For all we knew, those doors could be the threshold to a new dimension, spiriting the nuns off to heaven each afternoon, to be redeposited inside the convent the next morning by Jesus Himself.

The evening after school closed for Christmas vacation, Sr. Mary Athanasius invited my parents and myself to the convent to receive my award. My knees knocked as Dad knocked on the front door and I waited, listening to the muted sounds within and wondering, as always, what went on behind those closed doors. *Would I see any of the nuns in "civilian" clothes? When they took off their wimples, if they even took them off, did they have hair, or were their heads shaved bald as some of my classmates believed?*

I never learned the answer to that mystery. Sister Athanasius opened the door and ushered us into the adjacent parlor, where she offered us some freshly baked chocolate chip cookies and presented me with my prize: a genuine plastic statuette of God's Own Mother. When I put it in my bedroom, I discovered that it glowed in the dark.

Hail Mary, Holy Mary, Mother of God. Immaculate Mary. The Blessed Virgin, The New Eve, Queen of Angels, Bride of Christ, Madonna, Mediatrix, Star of the Sea, Queen of Peace.

Let's just say that Catholics have a thing about Mary. She has more titles than Tiger Woods, and the popes are always coming up with more.

Each culture seemed to have its own version of God's mother, none more popular than Mexico's Virgen de Guadalupe whose image emblazoned on that peasant boy's ragged cloak has gathered more devotion than both God and Jesus put together.

Mary had become the "poor person's God (or Goddess)." God the Father was up in His heaven stroking his beard, and Jesus was too busy saving souls, but Mary was accessible. For starters, you could talk to her in English, or whatever your native tongue was, rather than Latin, which was the official language of the God-focused rituals of the Sacraments. Her favorite prayer was the rosary. It was, literally, something you could get your hands around, your fingers worrying the beads as you prayed that simple circle. Each decade of ten beads reminded you of one of the "mysteries" of your faith, your salvation. Rosaries came as simple as beans or nuts hand-strung along a piece of sisal to those carved from crystal or forged of gold. They came in sizes small enough to fit into a pillbox all the way up to the three or four-foot versions the Sisters of the Holy Faith had hooked from the belt of their habits. Those rosaries looked like they could have been used as a weapon, but I never observed even the meanest nun using one that way. I'm sure it would have been a sacrilege had she done so. The Protestants may have had their bibles but we Catholics had Mary and our rosaries.

THE ACCORDION PLAYER

As I've already said, Protestants were the biggest challenge to our faith, though I'd only met one that I knew about. My Aunt RuNetta was a Baptist, and she didn't seem so bad, but because I knew her soul was in "im-mortal" danger, I took every opportunity to try to convert her. It should go without saying that I would never even consider having the slightest thing to do with a Protestant church. It was a big sin to even step inside one of those dens of iniquity, kind of like Lot's wife looking back at Sodom before being turned into a human salt lick (Genesis 19:26).

Just inside our church doors, near the holy water font, where you dipped your fingers and blessed yourself with the sign of the cross before entering the church itself, there was a rack full of pamphlets. Some talked about Catholic organizations one could join, where to send money to help the work of missionaries, and forms to fill out to get a Mass said (for a "voluntary" donation) to help get a deceased loved one out of purgatory. But most were tracts warning about the dangers to our Faith. One that I especially remember cautioned against even considering joining that thinly veiled Protestant organization, the YMCA. Just knowing Protestants or being around them constituted a "near occasion of sin" according to the Irish Sisters, whose experience with Protestants in their home country went far beyond theological hair-splitting.

You might not think that a door-to-door salesman would have much to do with Protestants or pose great risk to a seven-year-old soul, but give me a minute. In the 1950s, such salesmen were our Amazon. They sold everything: encyclopedias, life insurance, Fuller brushes, spices, and vacuum cleaners for starters. I don't think I'm making up a memory of a guy bringing a live pony around to sell pictures of children sitting on the pony to send to the grandparents. But the most memorable one was the fellow selling accordions.

"Ma'am, I am not selling a musical instrument. This is a true opportunity for your children. Learning to play one of these," his pitch went on, "will open new worlds to them, and provide better hand-eye coordination. They'll become more cultured. And maybe even famous. You watch the *Lawrence Welk Show*, don't you?"

Usually, my mother could say no to such roving merchandisers, mostly because she couldn't afford what they were selling. But this guy was good. "You pay nothing but a small deposit now. This fine instrument comes with free lessons beginning in two weeks right here in your neighborhood. Over the course of the lessons, the weekly payment will cover the cost of your child's new accordion. Isn't your child worth it?" Mother signed me up.

At first it was fun. After figuring out how to strap the thing onto myself, I played with the buttons on one hand and the little keyboard with the other. Then I realized that to get some serious noise to come out, I had to wave my arms to get the bellows to function. He was right about the coordination part. And, sure enough, two weeks later, when my mother dropped me off for my first lesson, the accordion man was there, along with a dozen or so other budding "Lawrence Welks" around my age.

But there was a problem. A big problem.

The accordion class was held in the basement of a small building a half-mile from our house. As I started to go downstairs, I saw the signboard on the white clapboard structure that stood above our classroom: "Church of God." *Church of God? This must be a Protestant church. Worse, a Protestant church that claimed that it, not our Catholic Church, was God's church.*

I couldn't believe it. My own mother had signed me up to take accordion lessons in the basement of a Protestant church. How could she? Didn't she care about my soul? Didn't she know about Protestants? Hadn't she listened to the stories I brought home from the nuns at school?

And now I was trying to figure out where middle C was with the Protestant version of God hanging over my head from the floor above. *I might as well sell my soul to the devil right now.*

Somehow, I made it through that first lesson, but when my mother came to pick me up, my trembling voice announced, "Mommy, this is a Protestant church. I can't come back here for any more lessons." But she had already paid a couple of installments on the accordion strapped to my chest. She promised to talk with the priest about it. His counsel was that I could continue my lessons if I stayed below grade and didn't go into the church itself.

Fortunately, for both body and soul, the bathrooms were downstairs. But the damage was already done. Either because my faith was not as great as the priest's, or my musical skills were lacking, or Mother's money ran out, my accordion career was mercifully cut short.

And I don't recall thinking about it right then, but this may have been the first time I was introduced to compromise. The priest, what I was going to try to become someday, had found a loophole, a way to live in the "real world" while maintaining the rigid church rules of black and white, heaven and hell.

THE ELEPHANT IN THE ROOM

"Mom come here. You just gotta' see this!" my neighbor Jim yelled to his mother in the kitchen. "The Meyers have an elephant in their living room."

Jim and his parents were our neighbors, directly across from us on Taft Street. Our houses were part of a new post-war development of identical three-bedroom, one-bath ramblers, a California version of Levittown. The houses, seemingly planted from seeds by the veterans housing program, were sprouting like the mandatory saplings in each front yard. The development was intentionally ordinary. Men returning from the horrors of war wanted to settle down, forget the unforgettable, get a regular job, and raise a family.

Our living room windows spied on one another all day long. Jim lived on the more "civilized" side of the street, where yard met neighbor's yard, and good fences may or may not have made good neighbors. We lived on the side that backed up to fields where cows were calmly chewing their cuds, unaware that they would soon become homeless, as Fairfield raced to become California's fastest-growing town.

Even fifty years on, Jim insisted he'd seen an elephant in

our living room window. That's how he remembered it, and nothing I could say would change his mind. I, however, have the photograph that my mother took that day, and it clearly shows five little boys hugging a pony, not an elephant. They're all in their Christmas "jammies," except for Martyn, who's clad only in his tidy-whitey underpants. In the background is a decorated Christmas tree, and if you look closely, you can see Jim's house through the window. My youngest brother promptly named the pony Black Beauty, which we shortened to Beauty, probably because she wasn't black.

"Merry Christmas boys. We got you your own pony," Mother had said when Dad brought the pony home in the back of his new Econoline van. Mother had persuaded Dad to buy the pony at the Dixon livestock auction. Mother had a pony when she was growing up and thought her (now five) boys should have one too. The fact that she grew up on a five-hundred-acre ranch and not in a housing development didn't seem to have mattered. In fairness, I think the photo-op was the only time the pony was inside the house, although I can't be sure. Most of the time, it stayed in our backyard until a neighbor reported to the police that she'd been bitten by a horse fly. After the story made the local paper, we had to board the pony out until we moved to our own acreage a few years later.

So, my friend Jim was wrong. There were never any elephants in our living room. Even if Mother, named after her father's circus elephant, had wanted an elephant in the living room of her suburban tract house, the stubborn rules of physics simply wouldn't allow an elephant, even a small one, to fit through any of the doors.

The elephants that Jim remembered were in our backyard.

I came home from third grade one autumn afternoon to find two elephants in the yard of our corner lot eating from bales of hay. On the side-street that dead-ended at our house, a couple of circus trucks with their faded lettering contained the rest of the menagerie: a pair of caged lions, an ostrich-like emu, and an extremely large boa constrictor. The animals were accompanied by a pair of two-legged creatures that my Uncle Rusty had brought with him: Kinney and "Sweetpea." Kinney was Rusty's right-hand man, and Sweetpea was the diminutive, octogenarian, elephant man whose weather-worn body had more wrinkles than his pachyderms. To watch him "work" his charges, whose weight class was twenty times his own, provided its own brand of comedy.

After our visit to Uncle Franco's circus two summers before, he'd operated another season in the American Midwest before he'd decided to see if the grass, and the money, were any greener on the other side of the border. Ring Bros. Circus went to Canada. I think the plan was to cross the Prairie provinces and railroad the circus across the Rockies before re-entering the U.S. through British Columbia and the Pacific Northwest.

They didn't make it. The troubles started even before they got to the Rockies. The circus suffered a "blowdown" in Gravelbourg, Saskatchewan. A storm caught them unawares and knocked the tent down, destroying poles, canvass, and some of the seating. But it didn't destroy the circus spirit. The home movie I have of the event shows undaunted people as Susie the elephant pushes and pulls trucks and Uncle Franco's Cadillac out of the muddy remnants of the performance site. Circus people don't give up, and that same movie shows them setting up in open fields, sans tent, for performances and then shows the entire circus riding over the continental divide on flatcars behind a diesel locomotive.

Even the foothills of the Rockies can be brutal on older trucks. As the circus wound its way out of the mountain range, playing to small towns in central British Colombia, the trucks began to break down, and some were abandoned. Unpaid performers kept leaving. I remember my mother getting collect calls from Uncle Rusty from places such as Prince George and Kamloops. It wouldn't surprise me if some of Dad's poker winnings found their way into a money order heading north of the border. Eventually, nothing was left except the remnant that ended up in our backyard. Uncle Franco and his Cadillac took off for parts unknown, so it was Uncle Rusty who showed up at our house. That's where the money—and the gas—ran out.

The menagerie stayed in our backyard long enough to establish our family's reputation with the neighbors. But before the mayor sent in the police or called for the National Guard, Uncle Rusty located some land and a metal barn to rent a couple of miles away over in Suisun City.

There really wasn't enough circus left to put on complete shows, so the latest incarnation of the Richards' family circus business served as an attraction for grand openings and sales events at car dealers and shopping centers. Starting at our local Ford dealer, Monez Ford, the little circus would offer a couple of acrobat tricks, and the elephants would perform. Suzie would lift my aunt aloft in her trunk while Bonnie, the younger and smaller of the pachyderms bellowed a cheer. The elephants were not mother and daughter, but everyone thought they were. The lions, Prince and Queenie, growled from their cages to add atmosphere. All the while, Chet Monez tried to sell Fords to customers who might otherwise go across town to buy a Chevy.

After the elephants had moved over to the barns in Suisun, we would go visit them every week or so. We'd take apples or oranges for treats, which the elephants would take from our hands with their trunks unless we were brave enough to place them directly in their mouths. What I most remember about the elephants was their eyes. Bonnie, who was only five or six years old, always had happy eyes. She seemed to be perpetually smiling. Suzie was markedly different. Her eyes were sadder, tired looking. But they also looked wise, as if she were the wisest creature in the room. It was as if she had seen a lot in her life and maintained a kind of resolve about it all.

"What's that?" I asked my uncle the day I saw a cumbersome metal contraption that filled the bed of the new Ford Ranchero pickup that he'd probably gotten in a trade with Chet Monez.

"That's a howdah," he replied.

"What's a howdah?" I asked.

"You'll see," is all he said.

A few weeks before, my uncle had taken the owner of Hawk's Welding some pictures of what a howdah should look like, along with Bonnie, the smaller elephant's "measurements," and had just picked up the contraption that was now taking up the bed of his pickup.

His idea was to train Bonnie to give children rides on her back, another attraction for the little circus. Now, no one had bothered to ask Bonnie the elephant what she thought of toting excited, screaming children around on her back, sitting in some irksome iron saddle. And, judging from her reaction the first time the empty howdah was strapped to her back, hauling kids around a parking lot was not her first career choice.

The phrase I most often remember Mother using was, "Take a chance, Columbus did." Now old Cristóbal's reputetion has taken a hit recently, and rightly so, though I suppose the spirit of mother's insight still holds true because it must have taken some courage to risk ocean storms, a potentially mutinous crew, and the uncharted waters. So true to her motto, Mother took a chance: she took a chance with the lives of her young sons.

One day she took us out to the barns, where the elephants now lived, and we became Bonnie's guinea pigs, our opinion as unasked as Bonnie's, so we had that in common. While Sweetpea held Bonnie's trunk and spoke quietly to reassure her, Kinney and Uncle Rusty hoisted us into the howdah from a stepladder, two per side.

"Be brave, boys," Mother called out to us from the safety

of the ground. "You're elephant trainers now. And hold on tight," she said, as she focused her camera.

The photo she took shows us manfully clinging to the newly painted sides of the howdah. The picture could well have turned out to be the last photo of Mother's young sons all in one piece had Bonnie gotten out of the wrong side of the bed that morning. Since I'm still alive, I can report the experiment a success. Somehow, Sweetpea persuaded Bonnie to carry her new cargo without too much complaint, and a new attraction was added to the little show.

Time or fear has banished most of the details of that ride from my memory except for one. Another of Mother's frequent sayings, when asked, "How are you?" was to respond with a "Well, I'm as fine as frog's hair. Now that's not as fine as elephant fuzz, but it's pretty darn fine." I don't know anything about frog's hair, but my memory can tell you that elephant fuzz is anything but fine. Rubbing Bonnie's head after that first ride was like caressing the business end of a scrub brush.

Even without looking over any neighborhood fences, I strongly suspected that we were the only ones to have elephants in our backyard. And after the summer on my Uncle Franco's circus, I had a feel for my family heritage and knew that at least one of my feet was firmly planted there. None of my classmates practiced riding baby elephants or spent their weekends selling peanuts and balloons on a tiny circus in shopping center parking lots. Paper routes or mowing lawns were the first jobs of most of the boys I knew.

But when I walked those short three blocks to Holy Spirit School on Monday morning, I entered "Catholicworld." Sitting at my desk, answering Sister's questions, and wearing my uniform, I was just like all the other boys, at least on the outside. But in my head, something was brewing, like a percolating coffee pot. "Catholicworld" had hold of my other leg and was pulling hard. It was immersive, swallowing me up, like I was getting repeatedly dunked in the waters of baptism.

Every day, as I slipped through the little-known passageway between the last two houses in my neighborhood and the school property, I always checked to make sure that my guardian angel made it through behind me. All of us Catholic kids had gotten guardian angels, either when we were born or when we were baptized—I'm not sure which. Our angels went everywhere with us to watch over and take care of us. Mostly, they kept the devil away, but they were also on the lookout for speeding cars, dangerous dogs, and the like. The angels were real—to us. A priest had once told a story about his own guardian angel. He was a fat little kid, and when he sat at his desk, he always skootched to one side, hanging part of one cheek over the edge, to make room for his angel. So, it wasn't just me.

Angels were just one of a host of beings that inhabited "Catholicworld." We Catholics had the saints. We had saints for everything you could imagine, and then some. On February 3rd we went to church and got our throats blessed with a pair of crossed candles to ward off coughs and colds in honor of St. Blaise. On October 4th we took our puppies and kittens to church to have the priest bless them on St. Francis's feast day. St. Maria Goretti, a recent addition (1800s) was one of the nuns' favorites. She let herself get killed rather than lose her virginity. Their other favorite was "The Little Flower," a.k.a. Theresa of Lisieux, who gave up the good life to become a nun.

And then the two biggies: St. Christopher, who kept everybody safe when traveling, and St. Patrick, patron of all things Ireland—home base for our priests and nuns. He ran the devil and all the snakes out of the Emerald Isle but was less successful against the English, who continued to harass the Irish people for centuries.

And, of course, the martyrs who died for the faith: hanged upside down, thrown to the lions, baked, broiled, and deep-fried. And, when nothing else worked, you prayed to St. Jude, the saint for helpless cases. And in case we forgot any saints, November 1st was All Saints Day.

Mary, God's mother, had too many feast days to count. She even had two whole months. May was Mary's month, filled with processions and floral crowning of her statue by a girl selected by a Sister. And then October, the month dedicated to praying the rosary, Mary's favorite prayer. All Catholic families were supposed to kneel on the living room floor by the coffee table and pray Mary's rosary after dinner.

God Himself was the absentee landlord of "Catholicworld." In real-time, here on earth, the nuns, and especially the priest, filled in for Him. They taught us what God wanted us to know and how He wanted us to behave. And they made and enforced all the rules. As is well known, their main tool was that famous Catholic guilt.

All in all, it was a very efficient ecosystem for growing new Catholics.

But I've left out the most important part.

At Holy Spirit School, the Holy Bible was not our bible. Our "bible" was the St. Joseph's edition of the Baltimore Catechism. It had all the questions and all the answers. On page 62 my copy had a picture of a couple on their wedding day, dressed for the festivities, holding hands, and beaming. The title beneath the picture said, "This is Good."

Turning the page, I saw a picture of a priest saying Mass and another of a nun kneeling in prayer. The caption? "This is Better."

Those two drawings said it all, the goal of "Catholicworld." And that's what kept pulling on my leg.

FAILING FIRST CONFESSION

By the time I made it to my First Communion, I was convinced that I wanted to be a priest.

But before Holy Communion came sin and confession. You couldn't go to communion with sin on your soul. You needed to go into the dark confessional, tell your sins to the priest, say you were sorry, and be forgiven. (This was another of the perks of being a priest: being able to forgive sin.)

Remember Fr. Murphy? He was the one on the other side of the screen in the confessional. He was the one you had to tell your sins to. It was supposed to be anonymous. But it was Fr. Murphy, the guy who could talk to God. He would know it was me.

Before we get to my first confession, a few words about sinning.

As the nuns explained it, there are two kinds of sin, at least for Catholics: venial sin and mortal sin. Venial sin is your "regular" sin, the kind you commit getting out of bed in the morning. Forget your morning prayers? Tell your mom you got all your homework done before watching TV? Kick your little brother on the way out the door? These were venial sins, the everyday kind. As Sr. Mary Loyola tried her best to explain for us, venial sins were like tiny black pinpoints on the soul, as if you touched a freshly sharpened #2 pencil to your lily-white soul each time you sinned. Even millions of these venial sins couldn't begin to turn it black. But one mortal sin? That did the trick every time. Your whole soul was immediately blackened like the coal in a pot-bellied stove; and, if you died before your next confession, you would go to hell for all eternity, joining the likes of Hitler, Nero, and the godless Communists in Russia.

Sr. Loyola's image created my first theological problem.

Where was my soul exactly?

I tried to bring it up in class one day. "Where is our soul, Sister? Can we see it or touch it?"

But Sister was a bit fuzzy with her answer. All that she seemed sure about was that "At the moment of conception (whatever that was), God Himself puts your immortal soul inside you."

Problem solved, according to Sister, and no other questions were needed. This also allowed for Catholics to believe in evolution. Darwin was fine as far as he went, dinosaurs and all that, but when it came to new humans, God's day of rest was over, and He got personally involved in creation again.

So, I had to solve the soul problem on my own.

Aware of some of the more obvious functions of human anatomy, I eliminated several possible locations. But I could discover no necessary biological function inside the human butt cheeks. It was a large area, larger for some than others, and certainly had enough room for a lot of pencil marks. For all I knew, a quick swat on the butt might even remove a few sins without going to confession. So, I spent most of my grade school career sitting on my soul.

You might not think a seven-year-old capable of an action deserving hell. But you would be wrong. Look at the Ten Commandments. Right there, it says that missing Sunday

Mass or eating meat on Friday is a mortal sin. It doesn't? Well, it should. Which is why the Catholic Church issued an addendum, with some more mortal sins including the two mentioned above.

Unlike venial sins, mortal sins must be purposeful. The three criteria for a "successful" mortal sin include that it has to be bad (as defined by the church); the person has to know it's bad (knowledge); and she has to do it intentionally (free will).

To complicate matters, the church taught that a human being wasn't capable of adequate knowledge and free will (ergo, no mortal sinning) until reaching the age of "reason" at seven years old. Unfortunately, our parish scheduled First Communion towards the end of second grade, giving most of us a few good months to do some serious sinning.

I lied (a venial sin). There is one more kind of sin: a sacrilege. It's still a mortal sin, but worse. It's like adding insult to injury. Example: you commit a mortal sin but don't tell the priest in confession and then you go to communion. Whammo—sacrilege!

So, this was scrupulous me at seven years old, preparing for my First Confession and Holy Communion. We went to Mass every Sunday, but I had missed once when my mother was sick (Dad was away at his National Guard training). So, it was bad—missing Mass (1) and I knew it was bad (2). But did I miss Mass of my own newly-minted free will (3)? After all my mother was sick (valid excuse for her) and we lived three miles from the church. But shouldn't I have at least tried to walk those three miles and find the church?

Maybe the best approach when my First Confession came along was just to confess; better safe than sorry.

But Fr. Murphy.

I would have to go into that black box and tell Fr. Murphy that I was a *mortal* sinner. For weeks I agonized. I kept flipping the nickel over in my head. Heads I sinned; tails I didn't. Even standing in line for confession, I hadn't decided. Heads: tell. Tails: don't. Down to four kids in front of me, heads won. I would get it off my chest. But kid number three got yelled at. Everybody in line could hear Fr. Murphy raise his voice. If I could have gotten out of line, I would have run all three miles home, but Sister was standing there; no escape. I decided to take my chance on eternity. Better hell than Fr. Murphy's wrath. I told myself one more time that it was not my fault. I forgave myself and spared the priest the trouble.

When the confessional door opened, and one of my classmates exited, Sister motioned for me to go in. It was nearly dark, dimly lit by some unseen light, so I could just make out where to kneel. As I knelt, the light clicked off leaving me in total darkness, in a little room about the size of an entryway closet, where guests hang their coats. I could hear murmurs, indistinguishable voices, as the priest heard the confession of another child on the other side. I waited, silently and blindly, trying to remember what I had been taught to say when it was my turn to confess.

I heard the door open on the other side, and then the dim light came on again as a screened window opened. A voice said, "Yes, my child?"—my cue to begin.

"Bless me, Father, for I have sinned. This is my first confession." I began to rattle off a few venial sins from a more-or-less pre-approved list the nuns had suggested. We had all been cautioned against confessing adultery and coveting anybody's wife, as these were "adults only" sins.

"I forgot to say my morning prayers twice." (At least, I was sure). "I fought with my brothers." (No number, as this was a daily occurrence). "I had a bad thought." (No specificity. The nuns emphasized this as a sin, although none of us kids knew what it meant.) "And I was late for Sunday Mass once." (Technically true, since I was late for the whole thing.)

"Is that all, my son?" he asked.

"Yes, Father," I said, anxious to get out of there as quickly as possible.

"For your penance, say three Hail Mary's and three Our Father's."

I started to stand up, causing the little light to go on again so I could see the outline of Fr. Murphy's face through the screen. "Just a minute. You need to make your Act of Contrition," he said.

I began, "O' my God, I am heartily sorry for these and all my sins..." as Fr. Murphy pronounced the words of absolution in Latin, "Ego te absolvo...." and I continued kneeling.

"You may go now," the voice said as the screen slid closed. As I left the confessional box, Sister congratulated me on making a good first confession and directed me to one of the pews so I could say my penance.

My First Communion day was wonderful. The girls looked like little brides in their white communion dresses and veils. We boys wore black slacks and white shirts. We each carried a new little prayer book and rosary: white for girls, black for boys. Before communion time we sang "Jesus, Jesus, Come to Me" and then lined up with our hands folded in prayer at just the proper angle, right thumb over left, like we had practiced with Sister. I was the shortest in the class, led the line, and was the first to receive communion, as if Jesus thought I was special. After Mass and a reception in the parish hall with passible good slices of cake and hot chocolate, my family and my godmother took me up to Twin Sisters Park for a barbecue and a hayride. It seems that each of the congratulation cards I got had a dollar bill stuck into it. If Jesus hadn't made me rich, I was close.

But then the doubts began.

What if missing Mass that day was a sin, a *mortal sin*? And now I compounded it with a sacrilege every time I went to communion? Was my soul getting blacker each time? Was that possible?

To complicate matters, my concerns about hell got tied up

with a fear of being sent to Juvenile Hall—kid jail. My memory is blurry, but I think it may have had something to do with marbles.

We played marbles a lot at recess. We started out with knocking standard cat's eyes out of a circle with our shooter and, following Sister's orders, at the end of recess everyone got their own marbles back, probably like Jesus did when he was a kid. But then, we discovered the fancier marbles—aggies, puries, boulders, and steelies—and started playing for "keepsies."

When even that got boring, some of the more creative, greedy, or entrepreneurial among us started building little devices out of cardboard shoe boxes and masking tape. They would use their mother's kitchen knife to make marble-sized cutouts in the box and build ramps inside, hidden by the lid.

"You wanna' win a steelie, or maybe even a boulder? Just drop one of your regular marbles into one of these slots and see what happens," the boys who owned the boxes would say. Then they'd drop a marble into a hole and not even two seconds later I'd hear a clink and a beautiful round shiny steelie marble (née a ball bearing) would pop out a chute at the bottom of the box. "Just like that. All there is to it." I never won. I always got a "better luck next time," as my classmate kept my marble.

I guess that one day a boy realized he was being cheated and told Sister. By the time the nuns got wind of what was going on, there were ten or twelve of these cardboard casinos, each more elaborate than the next, populating the playground during lunch recess.

I suppose it would have been a bit harsh to tell us we were all going to hell for gambling, what with the parish holding a weekly bingo game to help keep the school afloat. Instead, the nun smashed all the cardboard games with her black "nun shoes," confiscated all our marbles, and probably told us, "You boys are lucky I found this instead of the police. Gambling is against the law and they might have put you in juvenile hall, and even your parents couldn't get you out. All they could do is visit you once a week."

The point is, I now realized that grade school kids could not only go to hell, but they had a special jail just for them if they broke certain rules. For the next two years, I kept sitting on my soul and worrying about its salvation, especially if I got put into Juvie. I was miserable. Ghosts under the bed and monsters in the closet had nothing on my fear of hell. To add fuel to the fire, as it were, I had glanced up at the hot California sun one summer day and realized that that's where hell was: It was up in the sky and blazing hot. So now, had I ever doubted, I knew hell was real.

Something in my psyche has blocked out how I untied this Gordian knot. I don't remember ever talking with anyone about this. I certainly didn't tell the priest about it in confession. Maybe I forgave myself. Or I just got better at sinning. Or maybe, just maybe, this was the first chink in the armor of my blind faith.

And through all this, I still wanted to become a Catholic priest.

But why?

Why would a seven- or eight-year-old want to be a priest? Priests had to take vows: poverty, chastity, and obedience. They wore funny clothes at Mass and had to walk around in a long black dress the rest of the week. And the hat that some of the older priests wore, the biretta. It was just plain weird; a dull black, tri-cornered affair like an American revolutionary war soldier wore, except turned inside out. It was "traditional," probably designed by some pope's nephew who had flunked millinery school. And if they made you a bishop, it got worse. The hat you wore then, a "Miter," made you look like you were trying to turn yourself into a rocket ship or a God-seeking missile.

But speaking for my own seven-year-old self, things

looked a bit different. Not being able to marry? Having a wife was pretty much like having a mommy, I guessed, except you kissed her different. So that was no big loss.

And obedience? Well, I was already supposed to obey my parents, so I had practice, plus I didn't see anyone the priest had to obey. Seemed to me he was pretty much the boss of himself *and* all the people who went to church on Sunday.

And poverty? Even at seven, that was a stretch. The guy got a new car every couple of years and lived in a house a lot bigger than ours. And he got respect. And lots of Christmas gifts. And people invited him over for dinner.

But of course, we're asking the wrong question. A boy didn't "want" to become a priest. He was "called" by God. He had a "vocation" is what they said.

This "they" was an entire cottage industry within the Catholic Church dedicated to growing future priests. It started with mothers. Having a son who was a priest was the closest a woman could get to a guarantee of heaven, a first-class ticket. And then the nuns. Every boy they could recruit was another feather in their habit. Each diocese had a "vocations director," a priest whose only job was to create clones of himself. He'd give talks at the Sunday Masses in parishes; visit the older boys in Catholic grade schools; make sure the diocese had a functioning seminary; and of course, wine and dine the Catholic businessmen who footed the bills.

Still, there was something more. There was something that made you feel good inside, special, even if you were still just a little kid. It wasn't all the things you liked or didn't like about priests that you could see. Mostly it was inside you, a part of who you were.

Maybe it was what they said, a call. God's call.

Time would tell.

ALTAR BOYS

The first step on the road to priesthood was becoming an altar boy. I remember sitting in the front pew of the old Holy Spirit Church with a group of my (male) classmates. One of the nuns was standing in front of us, explaining how fortunate we were to have been chosen to serve at God's altar. Unsaid was how fortunate we were to have been born with a penis, which was a requirement for such service. That matter was brought up, indirectly of course, a few years later when our class was preparing to help with the dedication of the new church building. We, our whole class, including the girls, were going to stand on the altar steps—inside the altar rail, mind you—and sing a hymn during the dedication ceremonies. The nun, a different one probably, went to great lengths to inform the young ladies among us what a special privilege it was for someone with a vagina (she didn't refer to that term specifically) to be able to enter the sacred space normally reserved to the male of our species. And we all sat there, boys and girls alike, and took it in as if it were perfectly normal and proper, which at the time it was, I suppose.

Just behind Sister Mary Something or Other was that

barricade to the Holy of Holies, otherwise known as the altar rail. This barrier, about three feet tall, stretched the width of the front of the church, except for an opening that the priest and altar boys used during Mass to approach the altar. It is where the faithful came and knelt and stuck out their tongues to receive Jesus in communion near the end of Mass. The altar rail had a covering of white linen to catch Jesus if he slipped from the priest's hand while placing him (in the form of the consecrated bread) on the communicant's tongue, her open mouth waiting like a baby bird's. It was one of the altar boy's duties to ensure that the linen had been folded over the top of the rail before the communion service began.

The altar rail linen was just a backup, like the net the high wire walker used in the circus. The primary line of defense to prevent Jesus from hitting the dirt should the priest miss his mark was the altar boy himself via the gold-plated *paten* that he held under the communicant's chin just as the priest selected a thin wafer from the chalice-like *ciborium* and put it on a waiting tongue. This required considerable practice as well as an innate talent for walking backwards along the altar rail. And it required enough hand-eye coordination to hold the *paten* close enough to prevent the Host, or any crumb therefrom, from going amiss while avoiding interference with the priest's hand in the repeated dip and drop as he processed (walking front-ways) along the line of kneeling communicants. Most of the assistant priests were cool, but the pastor Fr. Murphy was intolerant of even the smallest bump against his hand or a waiting chin. A faux pas could result in being placed on the schedule for only the earliest morning Mass.

Lest the reader think I overstate, I once watched—from the pews, thankfully; I was not on duty—a consecrated Host drop to the floor.

Time stood still.

Breaths were held.

In some corner of heaven, a mark may have been placed

in a book.

Eventually, remembering his seminary training and the vows he took, the priest reached down between his feet, picked up the dropped wafer, and placed it in his own mouth. He then returned to the altar and grabbed the special cloth he wiped the *chalice* with; the one that had to be hand-washed by the ladies of the Altar Society; and wiped the floor where the wafer had fallen. The altar boy stood trembling, trying not to pee his cassock, while the remaining communicants prayed for his immortal soul. A favorite speculation among the altar boys was what would happen if someone got sick and up-chucked a Host, right there in front of God and everybody. *Would the priest have to eat that too?*

But again, back to the altar boy class. The first step to becoming an altar boy was to learn some Latin. The Latin lessons began with the prayers at the foot of the altar, a dialogic recital of Psalm 42. The priest began with: *"Introibo ad altare dei"* (*I will go to the altar of God*).

And the altar boys responded, *"Ad Deum qui laetificat juventutem meam"* (*To God who gives joy to my youth*). The Latin I was now committing to memory was the same as I heard "God" speak at my first Christmas Eve Mass but by now, fourth grade, I was hearing God talk to me in other ways, so the irony escaped me.

Over the next eight or ten weeks, we practiced this, and the rest of the Latin responses needed to get us to the Last Gospel at the other end of the Mass. We also learned other critical functions, such as how to hold that *paten* at communion, when to ring and mute the bells, and the proper technique for mixing just the right amount of water and wine in the priest's chalice. As one might imagine, this task depended on the individual priest's taste. Then there were the "back of the house" chores, such as laying out the priest's vestments in the sacristy, the room behind the altar where Mass preparations took place. And filling the cruets for the wine and water. If there is a sin somewhere between mortal and venial, it is likely sipping some of the altar wine back in the sacristy before Mass. Of course, it hadn't been turned into the blood of Christ yet, but still.

A particularly challenging task was lighting the altar candles. Since they were tall, we used a special lighter, available only from the church supply house in San Francisco. It featured a waxed wick that could be pushed through a tube to the right length. The extended end could then be bent as necessary to reach the candle's own wick, residing slightly below the brass cup, which kept the candles from dripping. While this was done before Mass started, it was always under the watchful eyes of the old ladies who came early to "finger their beads" and ask God what they were doing still being alive. You could almost hear their silent "tut-tuts" as you fumbled with the candle lighting, particularly the six-foot-tall Paschal candle used during Easter season. On more than one occasion, they lost their patience when some newbie threatened to set the church afire by trimming his wick too long, and one of them came up and finished the job herself.

These first training sessions got us up to daily Mass levels, meaning we got to try our new skills during the weekday masses at 6:30 or 7 a.m., where our only critics were the harshest ones: the priest and the old ladies mentioned above. Sunday high Mass with its incense and swinging *thurible* and holy water sprinkled on the congregation was reserved for the guys with more experience.

I cheated, sort of, in the Sunday Mass department. My dad was in the National Guard and spent one Sunday a month training at the old armory in San Francisco. Occasionally he let me go with him and explore the cavernous building while he did whatever he did—mostly talking to the other reservists, it seemed. As I recall, there were offices upstairs and a huge concrete or hardwood floor in the expansive ground-level space that could accommodate drilling platoons and even

Jeeps squealing their ribbed tires on the polished surface. One Sunday, just after I had finished my altar boy training, Dad took me along. Another reservist was there, a Lt. Colonel, a priest, and he invited me to be his altar boy when he offered Mass for the Guardsmen that afternoon.

Our "church" was the recreation room, and the only available flat surface for an altar was the pool table. We put away the cue stick and pushed all the balls into the pockets before the colonel/priest spread a white cloth over a section of the green felt. His portable "Mass kit," which he carried in a small satchel, contained all the essentials: a cross, missal, candles, chalice, communion wafers, and the obligatory wine along with his "vestments": a *stole* and a truncated *chasuble* which just barely covered his belly. I responded to all the priest's prayers and poured the wine and water into the chalice, but I don't remember there being any *paten* to hold during communion. The congregants stood around in their army green fatigues and polished black combat boots laced halfway up their calves. They were Catholic soldiers and required to go to Mass, probably by both the pope and their commanding officer.

In trying to refresh the details of my memory, I revisited that old armory in the Mission District of San Francisco. The sign on the gated front door indicated that I would have to call to make an appointment for a tour. The building was now owned by KINK.com, one of the country's premier(?) pornographic movie producers. I never got around to booking my tour but will forever wonder how that pool table was being used by the KINK people.

In the old days, before the changes of the second Vatican Council (1962–65), the Catholic funeral was downright morbid. Well, you for sure knew you were dead, at least. Everything was black: the altar veil, the priest's vestment, the funeral pall, the attitudes. A half dozen six-foot candles that smelled like death and somehow made me think of embalming fluid, flanked the casket at the altar rail like spectral pallbearers, ready to take the deceased to her spiritual resting place as soon as the service was over. The heavy odor of incense, probably necessary in earlier times for the survivors to live through the service, hung in the air. The musical accompaniment was the *Dies Irae* ("Day of Wrath") ponderously pounded out by an amateur organist.

We expected old people, upwards of forty or so, to drop dead on a regular basis, but I won't ever forget the first funeral Mass I served for. The deceased was a sixteen-year-old girl, an auto accident victim. It was a closed casket affair, but I heard enough scuttlebutt in the sacristy to get some lurid details of why: near decapitation, wax replacement lips, etc. I tried not to gag as I held that *paten* down by the altar rail, the closest I got to the casket with the dead girl. Fortunately, it was quick, as only a few people took communion.

My next brush with young death didn't involve my being an altar boy but it was more significant.

Construction sites are a delight for young boys: dynamic forbidden pleasures. One day there's a chance to sneak a handprint in wet cement, a stab at youthful immortality. On another the opportunity for alternative capitalism, collecting "nickel" knockouts from electrical boxes. Foundations with the rebar still sticking up become forts. Skeletons of houses begged to be the scene of ghost stories come alive. Each day a shifting playground for young ideas, the work that boys are meant to do. There's not a mother alive who, try as she might, can keep boys out of such a Shangri La.

When we first moved to Fairfield, the next street over from us was a farmer's field filled with gentle cows, contentedly chewing their cuds—ruminants ruminating, unaware that in less than a year, they would be replaced with bulls, the dozer kind. First came roads, then foundations, two-by-four skeletons, tar paper, and windows; all before the house could be closed in enough to keep us out on the weekends when the workers stayed home with their families.

My brothers and I fought wars, made deals, invented new worlds, frightened one another, and collected things from the bounty of construction debris; bits of wallboard to use as chalk, nails of all sizes and shapes, chunks of two-by-fours for making castles at home, and the prized "nickel" punch-outs from the electrical boxes, which made us feel rich and with which we tried to fool the coke machine down at the gas station.

But all good things must come to an end. The paint went on, and people moved in. Our new neighbors forced us to grow up. The time had come to put away the things of a child, as the good book says. The new houses came with new intrigues— girls. Maureen, with her smiling Irish eyes; Cheryl, on whom I had a crush (or was it her mother?); and the unapproachable, at least to me, Julie. It didn't take long to forget about our construction site.

Across town, a couple of years later, the scene repeated itself. Bulldozers, job shacks, deliveries of wood and concrete. And boys. Different ones this time, but really the same.

My mother had become a newspaper photographer, shooting lots of people with her speed graphic but never killing any. Early on she had taught me to help her in the darkroom Dad had built for her in our garage. And, as I got older, she'd take me on assignments with her. It was society stuff mostly, human interest they called it: shovel turning for the new hospital, school plays, one of the "brass" at the base getting another medal. That sort of thing.

But that rainy October day was different. She took me with her to a construction site. I mostly remember it being muddy and wondering, as I was holding her camera bag for her, why she was taking multiple pictures of an empty, muddy, hole in the ground.

When we returned to the same neighborhood later in the week, I found out. I saw something I'd never seen in my life. Nor wanted to.

This time we bypassed the construction site and went to one of the finished homes. That's where I met the three boys: Jaime, eight; his brother Carlos, six; and their cousin Tony, also six. They were identically dressed in their Sunday best. For little boys, they looked positively angelic: ruddy faces, almost too ruddy; hair slicked back, and not a strand out of place.

The two brothers shared a single coffin, lined in puffy white satin, shorter than adult size, but wider. Cousin Tony was laid out in his own, a foot away.

As we drove home, I noticed the new fence around the construction site's retaining pond.

That's where they had found them.

Why did my mother take me on such a frightful misadventure? She never said, never offered an explanation. Maybe, knowing where she was going, and why, she needed moral support herself. Or maybe she wanted to teach me a lesson. If that was it, it worked. It made me perpetually aware of that fine line, that few feet, that couple of milliseconds, between fun and disaster. But it didn't keep me from taking chances.

My first wedding—not mine personally—was a much happier affair, at least for me. I can't speak for the couple getting married. It was at Christmas time, just after the Holy Family had left the manger but before the poinsettias wilted. It was in the new church building, which was decorated in reds and whites which matched the bridal party's attire. Even the new cassocks the altar boys were issued for the new building matched: a deep crimson compared to the old sparse black. It was the first time I made any money for serving at Mass, so it opened a whole new world of possibilities for me.

Which brings us to the subject of cold, hard, cash.

The privilege of being an altar boy was meant to serve as its own reward, but there were a few "perks." One of the assistant priests took us on an annual altar boy picnic for a day of hiking and swimming, or over to San Francisco to see a

Giants game at the old Candlestick Park. And we occasionally got to skip class for liturgical services scheduled during the school day. This included First Fridays, Lent, Holy Days of Obligation, and funerals. Weddings and baptisms were always on the weekend, but the deceased usually forgot to plan ahead, so most funerals called us out of class to do our duty.

Completely unmentioned by the nun who provided our altar boy training were the tips we often got for serving at functions apart from Sunday or daily Mass, the aforementioned baptisms, funerals, and the granddaddy of them all, weddings. At weddings, five-dollar bills were not unheard of, usually dependent on the wildness of the bachelor party the night before. And once, one of the priests got so mad at the paltry participation in the collection basket one Easter that he threw all the coins out the back door of the church for a private Easter egg hunt for the altar boys.

***

I was afraid I was going to get drummed out of the altar boy corps just a couple of years after I started.

Before the Second Vatican Council, Catholics didn't have Bible studies or prayer groups. Our mid-week devotional was known as *Benediction*. It was a service of prayer and song centered around looking at Jesus, present in the holy bread. A wag once quipped that it took Catholics more faith to believe that the flat, round, plasticky tasting wafer was really bread than it took to believe that bread could be turned into Jesus's body.

Most of the time, they kept Jesus locked up, hidden in the golden *tabernacle*, sitting on the high altar. An eternal flame burned nearby to remind the faithful of the Lord's perpetual presence.

But on Wednesdays, the priest took Jesus out of the *tabernacle* in the form of the large white wafer (Host), identical to the one Father himself used at Sunday Mass, and placed Him

(Jesus) in the round window of a *monstrance*, an elaborate gold display case on a stand. In between two Latin hymns, *Tantum ergo Sacramentum* and *O Salutaris Hostia* and some prayers, the priest would hold up the blazing gold *monstrance* and bless the congregation with it as they murmured their prayers of adoration.

The priest's hands must have gotten dirty since Sunday when he held, prayed over, and then broke that same bread with them. Midweek, his hands were not allowed to even touch the gold vessel the Lord was displayed in. He wore a special vestment, a shawl-like affair called a *humeral veil* around his shoulders. It was long enough so that he could wrap his hands around the ends and pick up the *monstrance* that way.

I had a dog, or a dog had me. He was a pure white Samoyed Husky whom I called "Boy." Well, he was pure white until he stuck his nose into a bush one day and got sprayed by a skunk. It took me three large cans of tomato juice before either of us was even allowed back in the house. For several weeks afterward, his face was a dull red, as if the whole skunk incident had really embarrassed him. Boy had shown up at our front door one summer day and decided to stay. We were inseparable, and when he disappeared a year later, it broke my heart. One time, when I was an altar boy for *Benediction* services, Boy followed me to church. I told him to stay outside and made sure the door was closed.

But about the time the service started, Boy joined the congregation, not singing or praying, just sniffing around the pews and confessionals. As the priest was getting ready to bless the congregants with Jesus in the *monstrance*, Boy noticed me on the altar and bounded over the altar rail to greet me. Gasps ensued, giggles by some, as I tried to shoo my dog away with one hand while ringing the bells with the other. He trotted off, only to run behind the altar and re-emerge on the other side. Before I could die from mortification right there in

Jesus's presence, a couple of the men, maybe the only two in the congregation that included mostly the same older women who couldn't get enough church on Sunday, corralled Boy and took him back outside.

I was halfway out of my cassock and surplus before we reached the sacristy, and I headed for the door, hoping the priest wouldn't realize it was my dog. I guess he never figured it out, or maybe was a dog lover himself. I heard nothing about it, and the following year the priest approved my application to the seminary to study for the priesthood.

GOD GETS A NEW HOUSE

While I was in the sixth and seventh grades, God was getting Himself a new house. He needed it because we were outgrowing our old church. The last Christmas Eve before the new structure was finished, we only got to church in time to hear Mass in the parish hall. They had set up some folding chairs and put up a scratchy loudspeaker, so we could hear some of what was going on next door. Normally the parish hall was where we went to celebrate the Catholic church's eighth sacrament, Friday night Bingo. And, fortunately, the Mass was still in Latin, and the laity weren't required to make any responses to the priest's prayers, so nobody messed up and yelled "Bingo" after the consecration.

The new building was huge: so big it could have swallowed the old church two or even three times with room left over for dessert. Its skeleton consisted of a series of forty-foot high squared-off concrete arches, painted white. The arches were connected with aggregate concrete walls that had to be lifted into place with a crane. Before they put in the massive altar and the pews, the building resembled a warehouse more than a church. The front and south side featured a large, covered porch, as if God planned to sit in an oversized rocker after services on Sunday and watch the cars whiz by on Texas Street.

Inside, you could have played a football game, if God were into that sort of thing instead of confession and prayers, although an errant kick might have smashed the stained-glass window. The saints came over from the old church, but they looked kind of lost in the new building. I felt particularly sorry for St. Patrick and St. Joseph. Their statues had manfully dominated the old building, but they looked like little boys in the new one.

We got to watch the church being built for more than one full school year, its own kind of education. I remember the massive ductwork they used for the building's HVAC system and watching the workers install the chandeliers that hung from the ceiling, their twenty-five-foot length still ending far above the future worshippers' heads. Not even the bravest among us dared set foot on the actual construction site. It was not for fear of God's striking us down with a bolt of lightning but of what the nuns might do to us that held us at bay.

The best thing about the new church was that it sat right next to the school, a mere three blocks from my house, rather than three miles. The direct result was that we got a lot more calls out of class to do our altar boy duties. Even the "civilians," the girls and the fellows who were not altar boys—could count on some class cutting for the Stations of the Cross during Lent and Mass on the Holy Days of Obligation that occurred during the school year. The biggest was All Souls Day, where a required number of prayers practically guaranteed getting a dead relative out of purgatory and through the Pearly Gates. The catch was that there was only one soul release per church visit, so we spent the day going back and forth from class to the church, until we ran out of dead relatives. Now, this may not have been the official Vatican position, but it's how it came down to us.

About the time the new church was being built, two old men died, one in Rome and one in San Francisco. Even though I knew neither of them, their deaths would have a significant impact on my young life.

When Pope Pius XII died, the Cardinals (the "princes of the church") couldn't agree on who was to lead the church for the next decade or two. So, they chose a "caretaker," an already old man who would be expected to do little or nothing while the various factions competed for supremacy. The cardinals blew it. The roly-poly old man, Angelo Roncalli, did cooperate by only living for a few years. But, as Pope John XXIII, the worldwide council he called, Vatican II, shook the bedrock of Roman Catholicism more than anyone since Martin Luther in the sixteenth century. The changes initiated by Vatican II would radically reshape my years in the seminary.

Closer to home, 1961 witnessed the death of Archbishop Mitty of San Francisco. He was quickly replaced by the bishop of Sacramento, Joseph McGucken, but Pope John took the opportunity to reorganize California Catholics. The massive archdiocese of San Francisco was broken up with the creation of three new dioceses, or administrative regions: Oakland, Stockton, and Santa Rosa. Finally, our county, Solano, was switched from the jurisdiction of San Francisco to Sacramento. What this would mean to me was that my first five years of seminary would be spent in the backwater of Galt instead of the more cosmopolitan environs of the San Francisco Peninsula. It also meant that, if I became a priest, my first boss would be the new bishop of Sacramento, Alden J. (ding-dong) Bell.

Apart from its dedication, the first major parish event in the new church building was the Confirmation of my seventh-grade class. Confirmation was a bigger deal in Catholic grade school than eighth-grade graduation because God was involved. Not all of God, just the Holy Spirit. In Christianity, God comes in three parts: The Father (old man, gray beard); the Son (Jesus); and the Holy Spirit, the part of God after which

our parish was named. It was believed that, as the Sacrament of Confirmation was celebrated, the young person became a "soldier of Christ." Theoretically, I think, this made her a grown-up Catholic and probably willing to die for her faith, if it came to that. And it may have meant that the Guardian Angel we were assigned at birth was free to move on to a new client, but I wasn't sure about that. The image for the Holy Spirit was multiple choice: either a tongue of fire or a dove. On Confirmation Day, the girls got a little silver dove on a chain to put around their necks. I don't remember what the boys got to help them remember the Holy Spirit, if anything. I do remember that it was another one of those religious occasions where money came inserted into holy cards. Along with my tips from being an altar boy, my Catholic faith was beginning to pay off.

The other thing about Confirmation was that you got quizzed by the bishop about how well you knew your catechism, and he slapped you. This was not a quid pro quo. You got slapped no matter how well you answered the bishop's catechism questions. All this was a formality, a part of the ceremony. On my Confirmation Day the bishop asked four or five questions from volunteers, and the "slap" was a hand touch to your cheek; but the way the nuns prepared us, you'd think we might be taken directly to hell by Satan if we answered wrong, or that the slap might launch us straight to heaven. It scared us, and nobody looked forward to the ceremony. Well, none of the boys. The girls got to dress up and get their hair done.

The "other" other thing about Confirmation is that the bishop confirming us was the assistant bishop from San Francisco—we hadn't been assigned to Sacramento yet—named Merlin Guilfoyle. Merlin? Seriously, what were his parents thinking? But then, who am I to talk? The thing I recall about "Merlin the magician," as we called him behind his back, was that he was into the ring kissing thing. The proper way to greet a bishop in those days was to genuflect in front of him, take his hand, and kiss the jewel-encrusted ring that was one of the symbols of his office.

A few years later this same bishop had the misfortune of being the bishop of the Stockton diocese when that fine Irishman the Rev. Oliver O'Grady began his reign of terror in the good bishop's diocese. O'Grady was an equal opportunity abuser, showing no clear preference for boys, girls, or grown women. Bishop Merlin had the further misfortune of receiving a letter from O'Grady, admitting to one of his earliest conquests, an eleven-year-old girl. He simply transferred Ollie to another parish. Years later Bishop Merlin was undoubtedly still negotiating entry into heaven with St. Peter when several of O'Grady's later victims were awarded a cool thirty million from the Stockton diocese. Of course, neither I nor the bishop knew of any of this on my Confirmation Day, as none of it had happened yet. More on this later.

I have two photos from my Confirmation Day: in both, I'm wearing my bright red Confirmation robe. One is of myself and Bishop Guilfoyle. The other, the better photo, is of me and my churchgoing dog "Boy."

FINDING THE HOLY GRAIL

My mother was, to put it mildly, a packrat. It started with rummage sales, and by the time I was nearing the end of my grade school career she had graduated to the semi-annual U.S. Post Office auction, held in San Francisco. I never personally attended, but I guess it was nirvana for hoarders. In a large warehouse was bin upon bin of items lost, abandoned, or confiscated in the process of moving the mail through "snow, rain, heat, and gloom of night." Most of the mail might have gotten through that gauntlet, but not all of it. The bins—"lots," as they were called—were varied. Some might contain hundreds of the same items, greeting cards for instance. Others were complete hodgepodges of miscellany. Still others contained different items in an identifiable category, such as women's clothing, tools, or religious items. I don't know if the lots said more about the people who lost the items or the postal workers who sorted them.

One time my mother found and purchased the Holy Grail. In legend, the Holy Grail is the cup or chalice that Jesus used at His Last Supper with his apostles the night before he was crucified. Supposedly, it contained the wine the first time he changed it into his blood and is the model for the chalices Catholic priests still use at Mass every Sunday. Ever since, Christians have been searching for that elusive goblet. Knights of both round and square tables have dedicated their lives to the quest. They seem to have been looking for some solid gold, bejeweled cup, although it's doubtful that a first-century itinerant Jewish preacher would have had access to such a treasure.

The gift, sine qua non, that a newly ordained priest receives is his own chalice, quite often a gift from his parents and/or the parish he represents. The chalice Mother had purchased was gold or appeared to be. The church rule was that the chalice be made of gold or silver, and, if silver, the inside had to be gold plated. The surface that touched the precious blood of Jesus must be of the most precious metal.

At one of the Post Office auctions, Mother had chanced upon a box of religious articles, which contained a chalice, complete with its gold *paten* in its own velvet-lined case. She bought the lot, including the chalice, rosaries, prayer books, and two of the kitschiest icons I had ever seen: light-box portraits of Jesus and Mary displaying their hearts, his "Sacred" and hers "Immaculate." When the boxes were plugged in, the hearts appeared to be pulsating. Edgar Allan Poe would have been jealous.

When Mother showed me the second-hand, bargain chalice that would be mine on my Ordination Day, she explained her plan to trim the rim with precious stones—rubies, diamonds, emeralds—one for each of the twelve years I would spend in the seminary studying to be a priest.

Besides being gold-lined, every priestly chalice needed to be consecrated by a Catholic bishop in a special ceremony before even the precious gold was worthy to hold Jesus's blood at Mass. Considering how she acquired the chalice, Mother didn't know if it had been consecrated or not. Did it need to be consecrated again for her son? Unconsecrated and re-conse-

crated? Or, as in the sacrament of Baptism, provisionally consecrated if no one was sure?

To get the answer to her question, she did what every good
Catholic woman/wife/mother should. She took the chalice to
our parish priest. Fr. Carney was now the pastor of Holy Spirit
Parish, having been appointed by the bishop to replace Fr.
Murphy, who had retired to the mists of Ireland. After explaining how she had acquired the chalice and her plans for it, she
asked, "Father, what should I do about this? Do we go to the
bishop now or wait until my son is just about to be ordained?"

Unlike Fr. Murphy, who seemed to be God-in-a-cassock,
Fr. Carney struck one as more of an... "organization man."
Though taller than Fr. Murphy and theoretically a few inches
closer to God, his thinning brown hair simply lacked the
gravitas of Fr. Murphy's closely trimmed full head of gray: the
color of God's in the pictures. With Fr. Murphy you always
knew where he stood on matters of faith, on morals, or any
other subject upon which he chose to expound. Fr. Carney was
more circumspect, more of a pleaser, a "hem-haw" man. If
backed into a corner, he could come out with one of the
church's standard infallible answers, but it took a while to get
there.

He had been a priest long enough to earn his pastorship
and would celebrate twenty-five years of priesthood two years
later, but it's unlikely that Fr. Carney had faced this situation
before.

"Mrs. Meyers, I will consult the Bishop's office about this.
In the meantime, I need to keep the chalice here at the rectory.
As you know, only an ordained priest is permitted to touch a
consecrated chalice. And since we don't know, we need to be
safe." Mother assured him that she had admired the chalice
only from the comfort of its black case and left it with him.

That was Thursday.

On Sunday morning Mother let us sleep in and went to the
early morning Mass alone. The new church was right next to

our school, only three blocks away, so we frequently walked to Sunday Mass there by ourselves, just as we did to school every day. During the sermon Fr. Carney held up the chalice that Mother had entrusted to his care.

"Something very disturbing occurred in our parish this week," he said. "A parishioner somehow acquired this chalice that I hold in my hand; this chalice designed to hold the precious blood of Our Lord; this chalice reserved only to the hands of a priest called by God Himself. Did this family, one right here in our parish, think they could keep this in their home? Did they think they could use it for special celebrations? Pass it around the table at Thanksgiving dinner or a wedding reception?"

Mother, sitting a few rows back, was mortified. Tears formed in her eyes, but she tried to hold them back. In those days it was still a mortal sin to miss Sunday Mass, and the cheater's rule was that you had to be present from the time of the first scripture reading until after communion. Even though she was not permitted to take communion herself due to her irregular marriage to Dad, making myself and my five siblings technically bastards in the eyes of the church, Mother stayed through communion time, wiping the tears away before anyone noticed.

When she came home, she told Dad what Fr. Carney had done.

Dad was not a Catholic but was one of a handful of non-Catholic husbands who basically kept the church going. He had helped build the school and was one of the main fundraisers for the recently completed new church. When he did attend services, he was one of the men who stood outside the church doors, smoking, while the sermon was going on and then helped take up the collection, his long arms extending the even longer arm of the collection basket all the way to the end of the pew. Unlike the Protestants, who simply passed the collection basket from person to person, ours were always attended by a man who walked row to row. I don't know whether this was to prevent theft or increase guilt. If Martin Luther was wrong and good works can get you into heaven, then my dad was on the list.

Besides the previous pastor Fr. Murphy, the only other person who had godlike authority in my family circle was Dad. When my mother came home and told him what had happened, he was pissed. Besides volunteering to help an organization that wouldn't let his wife take communion because she was married to him, he was a regular participant in the Tuesday night poker games at the rectory, sometimes even letting the priest win, although not so often that he didn't make enough to pay our tuitions in the parish school.

The battle was joined.

Dad got dressed and drove his Lincoln down to the church before the next Mass started. While there were no witnesses, and no physical injuries were reported, Fr. Carney had met his match, and then some. There were no more sermons about the errant chalice, which returned home with my dad. And later that afternoon, Fr. Carney called and apologized to my mother.

THE BOY IN THE BEAUTY SHOP

Before Mr. Gutenberg had gotten his hands all ink-stained, most Europeans were unlettered and got their education, religious and otherwise, from storytelling and various arts: sculpture, architecture, music, painting, and drama. A favorite was the "passion play," a dramatic presentation of the key moments in the final week of Jesus's life. It was a good story: suspense, blood, gore, victory for the good guy—but no sex.

The passion plays were based on the Gospels and followed the same basic storyline, but variations were allowed. Well after books were commonplace but before we were burdened by movies, television, and their digital offspring, new versions of the old story were being penned. One such was *The Upper Room*, written by the Rev. Robert Hugh Benson in 1914. He recounts the last events of Jesus's life through a series of reports given to the owner of the "upper room," where the Last Supper was said to have been held. The narrator, who took the lead role in the play, was his servant boy Samuel. The key events of the passion take place behind the scenes through sound effects or tableaus such as the Crucifixion and Pieta.

Enter my dentist, Dr. Philip Rashid, a diminutive Lebanese

American Catholic with a dramatic flair. He wanted to direct and produce a passion play, Benson's *Upper Room*, in our town during Lent—but not just for Catholic parishioners. He reserved the rarely used auditorium, fully rigged with seating around a thousand, that sat across from the county courthouse. He went first to Sr. Mary Athanasius, the principal at Holy Spirit School, to see if he could find an eighth-grader with enough acting skills to carry the lead role of Samuel. They selected a tall beanpole of a boy named Michael Finnerty.

But Dr. Rashid also scheduled open auditions. I had just come off starring in our seventh grade Christmas play, an adaptation of *Amahl and the Night Visitors*. I originally had a lesser role, but the lazy lead neglected to memorize his lines, and I was promoted. Having just been bitten by the acting bug, I tried out for the only role in the *Upper Room* that seemed to fit me, the servant boy Samuel. After hearing me audition, Dr. Rashid found himself facing quite a dilemma. I was clearly better than the eighth-grader he had already selected for the role, but he had committed both to Sr. Athanasius and to the Finnerty family. Also, I was only about four foot ten and appeared more like a child than an older teen or young adult. Mike was easily a foot taller. To add to Dr. Rashid's soul searching, he was short himself, often having to stand on a step stool to treat his patients. He auditioned both of us several times and had me stand next to the actors who would fill the adult roles. He agonized but eventually stuck with his choice of the eighth-grader. I was assigned to be his understudy.

Dr. Rashid was a fanatic. Even though his cast and crew were all amateurs, he demanded perfection. Although the play was religious and a bit on the melodramatic side, it was the most professional production our little town had ever seen. Five or six performances were sold out and a reprise was a natural for the following Lenten season.

With myself now in eighth grade and the Finnerty boy off to high school, there was no question who would play the lead part the following year. I hadn't grown much, but my size was overlooked in favor of my acting ability.

I'm probably the only kid who ever had his braces temporarily removed to perform in a town play. My director—and dentist—persuaded my orthodontist to temporarily remove my braces for the performances and reinstall them afterwards at no cost to my parents. Professional courtesy and all that. It was a pain, but not the worst part of my acting career.

I had to go to a lady's beauty salon to have my hair permed for the role, per Dr. Rashid's instructions.

"We're here for our 3:30 appointment," Mother told the receptionist.

"Name, please."

"Nove Meyers."

"And how do you spell your first name, Mrs. Meyers?"

"Oh, the appointment's not for me. It's for my son. He's Nove, N-o-v-e."

"For your son?"

"Yes."

"And you want him to have a... perm?"

"Yes."

"A perm? For your son?"

"Yes. Well, you see he's in a play. He's the star of the play. It's about Jesus. Maybe you've heard of it, *The Upper Room*. It's going to be at the theater across from the courthouse this weekend. And his dentist wants his hair permed for the part."

"His dentist?"

"Yes, well his dentist is also the director of the play, Dr. Rashid. His office is just up the street, over by Holy Spirit Church."

The receptionist called to the back of the shop. "Maria, can you take this one?"

It took hours. I got shampooed, had my head drenched with some god-awful smelly stuff, and had my surviving hair put in curlers. Finally, as if my budding manhood hadn't suffered enough, I got my head baked in one of those machines that look like they're going to transport you to a different dimension. Which would have been best if any of my school-mates had walked by the windows that showed the whole world the tortures that were going on inside.

My worst fear was that one of the girls in my class would come in with her mother to get her hair done while I was sit-ting there in curlers.

"God, take me now." It was pure psychological torture. It's doubtful I've recovered. Who knew that Jewish servant boys in 33AD had their hair permed?

The play was again a rousing success and got rave reviews.

One more twist. It turns out that Dr. Rashid's cousin was none other than Danny Thomas, the Hollywood actor and star of the then-popular TV show, *Make Room for Daddy* (1953–64). He was also the father of Marlo Thomas of *That Girl* fame. Of most real and lasting importance, the year prior (1962), Danny Thomas had founded St. Jude's Research Hospital for Children in Memphis. This hospital never charges families for its services; its staff has included a Nobel Laureate; and over the last half-century, St. Jude's has significantly improved the survival rate for children with leukemia.

Dr. Rashid was unsuccessful in getting his famous relative to come to Fairfield to see our production, but rumors were floating around about Danny Thomas producing our play with me in it in Hollywood as a high-dollar fundraiser for St. Jude's Hospital. Could even be the start of an acting career. Maybe I was on the verge of becoming famous. The conversations got as far as a meeting with Mr. Thomas at one of the big hotels in San Francisco, but no road trip to Hollywood ended with my name in lights.

Since I was only months away from starting my studies for the priesthood, this possible near-miss with fame proved another of those *what if*s that seemed to keep following me like the guardian angel the nuns had convinced me was hovering, ever unseen, over my right shoulder.

PART II

THE PRIEST FACTORY

GOD'S BOOT CAMP

I leaned against the massive chapel doors of St. Pius X Seminary, watching Dad's green Ford van recede through the row of eucalyptus trees lining Twin Cities Road. After the van had disappeared like the green dot that flashes just at sunset over the ocean, I found my way back to my dorm. I sat on my bed, identical to the dozen or so others that filled the room, except for the pattern of my bedspread. Mother had spent most of the last two hours fussing over making my bed and putting my clothes away in the nightstand and the small locker at the end of the room. She was not normally a "fusser," but she delayed leaving her firstborn in his new world, one she didn't control.

I lay back on the bed and shut my eyes. I was where I had wanted to be ever since I'd learned that going to the seminary was how a person got to become a priest. I was thirteen and leaving home, fearful and excited, in equal measure.

I was Daniel at the lion's den, a Christian entering the Coliseum. I was Don Quixote, fully armored astride my faithful steed ready to take on the largest windmill. I could see myself on the altar transforming the bread and wine into Jesus's body and blood with my words, "Hoc est enim corpus meum—this is my body." All that separated me from that moment were twelve years in the seminary: my lifetime again.

"Hi. I'm Bob."

I opened my eyes to see a tall, skinny guy with a blond crewcut standing over my bed. This was the first seminarian I met, other than the two classmates, Joe and Sabia, who had come with me from my grade school.

"You must be Nove, right? They sent me to look after you, show you the ropes. I'm supposed to be like your 'Guardian Angel' for a few days until you know your way around here."

"Yes, I'm Nove. Good to meet you."

"I'm a sophomore, from Sacramento. Would you like to take a tour of the place?"

"Sure. They gave us a quick tour when we came for the test, but it's a little blurry. So much to see, and I was concentrating on getting the test answers right."

"Where do you want to start?"

"I don't know. Anywhere, I guess. Only place I know is my dorm here and the office."

"Well, let's start with the gym and the pool. Most guys like that. By the way, where're you from?"

"Holy Spirit, in Fairfield."

"Oh. Very end of the diocese. You guys just made it in. A little further south, and you'd be going to the old seminary down by San Jose. You'd miss this nice new place we have here."

"Yeah, that's what they told us."

"Who's your pastor?"

"Fr. Carney. And before that it was Fr. Murphy."

"And the assistant priests. Who were they?"

"Well, we had Fr. Finnegan and Fr. Gallagher and a couple I don't remember."

"Notice anything about them? The names? They're all Irish—FBI, short for 'foreign-born Irish.' Most of the clergy in our diocese are Irish from Ireland. That's what makes Sacramento a 'missionary' diocese. We don't have nearly enough native clergy, priests, or nuns, so they import most of them from Ireland. Technically, that makes our diocese like Africa or China. That's why we have this new seminary. It's kind of like a factory for priests."

"Hmm. You're right. I knew the nuns in our school were from Ireland because they all talked about it, but I never thought much about the priests before now."

Bob led me out through the dorm past the communal shower room that separated my dorm from an identical one at the other end of the hallway. Before we got to the gym, he told me to look outside the windowed hallway to the right.

"See that space, with the markers on the ground? That's where they're going to build another dorm. If you notice, the north to south buildings are two stories. They're for sleeping. There's three right now. Your dorm and the one next to it are for students. The one past the chapel is for the priests and brothers. It's not really a dorm. They have individual rooms. At least that's what I'm told. Nobody's allowed to go over there."

"Why are they adding on already? I thought this place was brand new."

"Two years old, but I think that the dorm was planned originally. They just didn't know they'd have to add it so soon. I heard you guys have over sixty in your class. That's huge. Biggest group that's ever come to the seminary. It's because our diocese is growing so fast, and they're pushing to make more priests. Plus, we get the guys from the two new dioceses, Santa Rosa, and Stockton. You'll have guys in your class from Modesto, Turlock, places like that. Probably even up near Eureka, where the seminary used to be before they built this new one here in Galt. They did it right. Planned it to take care of the priest need for the next century or so. Several hundred acres here. Lot of room for expansion. Before long there will be plenty of native-born priests. And you and I, we're the beginning."

(At the time, that's certainly what it had seemed like, but Bob was wrong. The seminary went out of style sooner than the circus. St. Pius, built for a century, closed fifteen years later, having produced fewer than two dozen priests).

"Well, here's the gym. Other than the dorms, it's the only two-story building. The single stories are for classrooms. Oh, and the chapel. That's tall, nearly three stories. It has to be that big because some fancy artist in Paris built a huge stained-glass window for it."

"Wow. Nice gym. And big. What are the curtains for?"

"Oh, that's where the stage is. We also do plays here. Every Lenten season we have a Passion Play. You know, about the end of Jesus's life."

"Oh, I know about Passion Plays. I think I still have curls in my hair from the one I was in last year. I'll probably skip being an actor. Once was enough."

"Anyway, it's a big deal. Everybody comes, parents and all. Almost all the students are involved; actors, stage crew, ushers, you name it. Fr. Nick, he's our music teacher, he's the director. You'll meet him soon enough. Can't miss him. I mean that literally. You can't miss him. He's a big guy, biggest priest here.

"Weird thing, though," he went on, "about the play. Since everybody here at the seminary is a guy, all the actors are guys, even the girl parts. There's only a few though: Jesus's mother Mary, Veronica, and Mary Magdalene, I think. They're not speaking parts. Veronica just stands there holding her veil and Jesus's mother holds Him after they take him down from the cross. I don't remember what Mary Magdalene does. But here's the thing. Fr. Nick is talking about doing a fall musical—*Finian's Rainbow*, *Oliver*, stuff like that—which will have talking girl parts. Not sure how that's going to work out.

"Well, here's the pool. It's nice. You a swimmer?"

"Yeah, I learned in second grade."

"That's good. And I hope you learned how to hold your breath. They like to dunk people here, especially freshmen. Hold you down till you think you're gonna drown and then let you up. The meaner ones do it again. You have to watch out for that. Otherwise, the pool is fun. We play 'Marco Polo' and other games.

"We don't have time right now to explore all the grounds, but out back there are auto and carpentry shops run by the brothers, a pool hall that also has ping-pong tables and way out back, a shooting range. One of the brothers keeps everyone's rifles locked up and brings them out when a group wants to go practice."

"What do you mean when you say 'brothers,' Bob?"

"Well, there are some other men who live here at the seminary. They're not priests, even though they dress the same. I don't think any of them teach, but they might. They oversee the grounds, keep the cars running, and lots of other little stuff it takes to keep this place going."

"But they're not priests?"

"No. Mainly they can't say Mass or hear confessions. That's the big difference. I don't know why they are 'brothers' instead of priests. Maybe the Latin was too hard for them. Maybe God just didn't call them to priesthood. I guess you can ask them after you get to know them. Most of them are nice, a little quiet, but cool."

Next, Bob took me down a couple of corridors and showed me the classrooms, music room, labs, and the library. Finally, we got to the chapel.

"I'll take you inside and we can look around. Can't talk in there, so we'll come back outside, and you can ask me questions."

The chapel was like a big letter "U" laid on its side with the bottom of the "U" holding the altar and this huge stained-glass window of Jesus and his disciples. It was faced so the sun blazed through the window when we came for morning prayers and Mass. Pretty impressive, even if a person isn't a Catholic. There were confessionals in the back, near the big doors; an organ up front, but no separate choir loft as far as I could see. The strange thing, though, was that instead of statues of Mary and the saints, there looked like there were four or five more altars besides the main one, scattered throughout the building.

"Why are there so many altars, if that is what they are?" I asked Bob after we exited.

"Oh, those are side altars." He went on to explain how every Catholic priest in the world is obligated to say Mass every day, not just on Sunday like the rest of us. This reminded me of the nuns telling us about the priests locked away in Communist prisons who had to save or steal a crumb of bread and then sneak in their Mass when the guards weren't looking.

"We have about a dozen priests here at St. Pius," Bob went on, "and they each have to say their own Mass. So, each morning, while we are praying, meditating, and having our group Mass, you'll see individual priests, usually with one altar boy, coming out from the sacristy and going to one of those altars to say his own daily Mass. They're fast though. One of them can get through it in under fifteen minutes."

"I see that the organ is up front near the altar and there's no choir loft?"

"That's because we're the choir. Everybody sings. It's all in Latin. Well, it's about time for dinner. Let's head across the courtyard to the refectory. That's what they call the dining room. Not sure why, that's just what they call it. Kind of like it being the 'mess hall' for the military."

As we crossed the open courtyard, Bob pointed out a koi pond with a white statue rising above the goldfish. "That's Pius X, Saint Pius the Tenth, the one the seminary is named for. He was the first pope of the twentieth century. They made him a saint, probably because he made it so kids could start going to communion when they were seven instead of waiting until they were teenagers."

The dining hall was full of guys, new ones trying to figure out what to do, where to sit, and others renewing friendships after the summer. The rectangular tables each sat eight. Bob took me to one and stood me behind a chair. Everyone was still standing. Bob introduced me to the guy at the head. "Nove, this is Mr. McFadden. He's a senior. We call the seniors 'Mister.' He is the table proctor. He makes sure that everyone behaves and eats their food."

Did I mention that I was a picky eater? I hadn't planned on this part. It was my first brush with seminary reality. I know I didn't expect to survive on communion wafers like some of the saints the nuns had told us about, but I hadn't really considered the food part. Probably best, or I might not have signed on. In grade school, lunch had consisted of one of my two favorites, either a salami and cheese or a PB&J sandwich. I won't say that I eschewed vegetables entirely, but I chewed very few of them, and there were several hundred food groups not on my preferred list.

The table proctor (dictator) had other ideas. He insisted that we eat everything on our plate, recognizable or not. This was okay at breakfast, especially on French toast days with their vanishing slices of one of the few items we praised the kitchen for. I'd say they were just this side of delicious, but we wolfed them down like a pack of dogs, hardly taking time to taste them. I was a small kid and only managed eight slices on my best day, but I believe the record was twenty-two. Dinner was a different matter. The seminary treasurer Fr. Tim was the original gleaner. One story has it that the train that passed by two blocks from our classrooms spilled a load of tomatoes. That explained for me the months of stewed tomatoes that seemed to accompany every evening meal, as if the tomatoes were "getting it on" in some dark corner of the pantry and producing stewed offspring overnight.

You either ate the food that was provided, or... you ate the food that was provided. If you balked, you might also get a special assignment, such as writing a five-hundred-word essay on the sex life of the eggplant. My picky appetite was one of the first casualties of my seminary career. Those iron-rich tomatoes soon provided an iron lining to my stomach.

After dinner that first evening, one of the priests showed us a movie. I guess it was to help us not feel homesick or something. It was a World War II film. I'm not sure it helped with the homesickness, but at least there was popcorn.

***

The next day was freshman orientation day. The first part of the day went okay. After our morning rituals in the chapel and a passable breakfast, we got our textbooks for various classes and learned where each one met and when. Our "Guardian Angels" were around, plus some of the other priests who would be our teachers.

After lunch they crammed all sixty-three of us into one classroom. Guys were sitting in chairs, on desks, and on the heater registers along the wall. A few latecomers were standing. The same priest who showed us last night's movie came in. He walked to the front of the room and stood on the dais where the teacher's desk was. The six-inch dais made his own 6'3" frame even more imposing in the long black cassock he wore. He had the bearing of a military general, chiseled features, and jet-black hair, thinning on top, although I had to take others' word for that because at five feet zero inches, I couldn't get a bird's eye perspective.

Some things are a blur, but the next hour went something like this.

"What do you do when a priest walks into the room?" were the first words out of his mouth.

Silence. Finally, one voice ventures a guess. "We stand

up?"

"That's right. You stand up. And what do you say?"

No answer.

"You say, 'Good morning, Father.'"

"But it's afternoon," a voice from the back blurted out.

"A wise guy. Stand up. What's your name, son?"

"Michael."

"Michael, what?"

"Michael Patterson."

"That's not what I mean. When I ask you your name, you say, 'Michael, Father.' That's the right answer. Now Michael, you know so much about time, you want to be our time-keeper? You want to get up extra early to ring the bells to wake everybody up in the morning?"

"No."

"No, *what*?"

"No, Father."

"That's better. Sit down. Now, let's try this again. I'm going to go out and come back in." He left the room and re-entered a few seconds later.

We all stood up and said, "Good afternoon, Father," as he returned to the dais.

"Much better. I'm Fr. Luke, Fr. Luke McArthur. I'm the Dean here.

"Any of you know what 'Dean' means? It means I make the rules.

"You know what else it means? It means you follow my rules.

"Look around this room. Any of you see your mommies here? No, you don't. That's because they're not here to take care of you, pickup after you, mollycoddle you. Look outside those windows. Any of you see a truck outside with 'Janitor' painted on the side? No, you don't. And you never will.

"Here at St. Pius, we clean up after ourselves. We make our beds, sweep the floor, take out the trash, do the dishes, wash the windows.

"Here's the first rule. Each morning after breakfast you'll have a few minutes to make your bed. When I was in the army our sergeant used to check to see if we made our beds to regulation. He'd walk up to each bed and drop a quarter on it. If the quarter bounced, we passed. If not, we had to remake the bed. Here in the seminary, I use the same procedure. With one exception. I won't bounce a quarter on your bed. I use a feather."

Thus, began my lifelong hatred of bedmaking.

"Your dorm rooms are where you sleep, change clothes, and clean up. You don't go in there to sit, fool around, or eat. No food in your dorm. We're raising priests here, not packs of rats, so we don't want you feeding them.

"Anything that can't be done on a daily basis is saved for Wednesday afternoons when we don't have classes. The harder jobs, cleaning the toilets and stuff like that, is for my 'work crew' guys, the ones who forget about any of my rules."

There were no pins dropping in the room because we would have heard them. I looked down and took in a deep breath. When I looked up again, Fr. Luke was still there. But now I see him dressed in battle fatigues; his rifle slung across his shoulder; its bayonet rising above his steel helmet; pineapple grenades hanging from his camouflage vest, like the troops in the movie last night.

"I wasn't always a priest, you know. I didn't start out in the seminary like you guys. I found God in a foxhole in France during the Battle of the Bulge. That was us in the movie last night: the 101st airborne, the *Battling Bastards of Bastogne*. You know what happens if you're late getting into your foxhole?

"You get your effing head blown off, that's what.

"That's my next rule. Don't be late. No excuses. We have bells here. They tell you when to go to sleep, get up, study, pray, eat. Everything except when to take a piss."

Fr. Luke went on like this for another hour. I had so many rules spinning around in my head they were running into each other.

His final threat was, "And if any of you even think of bending one of my rules, may God have mercy on your soul." He pointed to the chalkboard behind him. "There will be crap and blood—yours—all over these walls."

Finally, the assault ended; and, as with all seminary activities, except possibly getting a haircut in the student barber shop, the gathering ended with a prayer.

Mine was getting out of this place alive.

Holy crap. What had I gotten myself into? This wasn't what I'd bargained on. I had never heard a priest talk this way. No priest I had ever known used curse words. And now here was this guy wearing a Roman collar and claiming to be a priest, threatening me to within an inch of my life, on the remote possibility that I would do anything wrong, and saying words that my mother wouldn't allow within a block of our house. In an hour, Luke McArthur had shattered my lifelong idea of what a priest was.

The quitter's phone was in a booth right next to the office, but for reasons known only to God, I kept the nickels in my pocket and walked past it that day, and the next, and every other for eight years.

***

Our regular schedule began the following morning.

BRRRRRRRRING. BRRRRRRRRING, followed by about a hundred ten thousand-watt fluorescent lights blasting on. It was 5:30 in the morning: time to get up.

Fr. Luke had told us about the bells, but I guess I'd expected something like the bells of St. Mary's or some other angelic chime welcoming us to another day on God's green earth. No, St. Pius seminary seemed to have gotten hold of some surplus fire station bells, the kind that not only roused the firemen from fireman dreams but ejected them from their beds and halfway down the firepole before their eyes were opened. We had fifteen minutes to throw on our clothes and splash water on our faces before the next air raid alert warned us that we had five minutes left to get our butts into a pew in the chapel.

Chapel time began with morning prayers. Like most, I was never awake enough to remember their content. Next came "meditation." This was a developed skill, requiring some practice to sleep with one's eyes open. And then, personal spiritual reading. The default spiritual reading classic was Thomas à Kempis's "Imitation of Christ." I guess that the essence of imitating Christ is sleeping because that baby would send any adolescent to dreamland no matter how badly he wanted to "do what Jesus did."

Fortunately, I found an alternative text in Thomas Merton's *The Seven Story Mountain*, his memoir about becoming a Trappist Monk. Merton was a "rebel with a cause." It was said of priests that they were to be "in but not of" the world. Merton was "in, but not of, the monastery." After a youth that would make Augustine blush, he became a monk but continued to push the boundaries in both his writing and travel. At the time of his death by electrocution—accidental not judicial—he was in Asia exploring a synthesis between Christianity and Eastern religions. But at least his story kept me awake. And a few years later, when I was in college, I would briefly flirt with becoming a monk instead of a regular priest.

Following this, we had song practice. It was Gregorian chant. Our songbook was the "Liber Usualis." We translated the Latin title loosely as "useless book," although it made a decent door stop. It had to have been fourteen inches thick and I swear it weighed at least twenty pounds. I think Latin words and the square musical notation of Gregorian chant must weigh more than regular music.

Of course, it could have been that every Tom, Dick, and Mary saint had their own feast day and about ten pages of music to go with it. A few years later, after Vatican II, they threw out about half the saints after discovering that they had never really existed; they were pure holy myth. It didn't upset people much, as it did simplify matters. All except for St. Christopher. When they found out he was just a legend and downgraded him to just "Mister" Christopher, it shook a lot of people's faith. He had been the patron saint of travelers and probably got prayed to more than anyone except Mary. God even. This is not to mention the havoc this wrecked on the holy medals business and the traffic safety people. I think they started putting seat belts in cars about the same time they downgraded St. Christopher.

The choir director was Fr. Nicholas Thomas Freund, a Friar Tuck clone without the joviality. Nobody pointed this out or called him "Nick Tommy" to his face. He was the one Bob had told me about. Fr. Nick wore the same black cassock as the rest of the faculty, except in triple X size. It was held on his massive frame by a cincture made of rope. His favorite extracurricular activity was to whack errant students with its knotted ends. He did it for talking in class, not singing loud enough, falling asleep, or for no reason at all.

At about seven o'clock, daily Mass would begin. By this time, even the priests were tired of praying, so most days Mass moved at warp speed. The record was twenty-one minutes, I think. As a reward for our perseverance, God treated us to breakfast, nearly two hours after that first infernal clanging that roused us from our dreams.

Thankfully, the tortures of the Inquisition in the Catholic Church ended some time ago. Except for one. That would be Latin class: six, yes six, days a week at 8:30 a.m. Fr. Justin Pierce was the resident Latin scholar at the seminary, and I'm sure that he was at least distantly related to either Queen Isabella or Torquemada, her first grand inquisitor. Each morning, save the Lord's Day, he would put the linguistic thumbscrews to us while we were still trying to digest our breakfast.

Had Cicero and Virgil foreseen how Fr. Justin was going to flog us with their texts a couple of millennia hence they might have left their styli in their holsters or at least used a version of the vernacular less complex than the emperor's Latin. Out of the entire class, only two people understood Latin: Fr. Justin and Matt Walker. For the rest of us, once we got past the equivalent of "See Dick run" which was "puer... something or other" with an "amo, amas, amat" thrown in; it was all Greek to us. Fortunately for Matt, he was quite bright, since he had to use up most of his own study time helping the rest of us with the next day's translation. We scored when we got to the *Aeneid* because somebody found a "pony": an interlinear translation at a used bookstore in Sacramento. This gave Matt a break and enabled most of us to pass the dread subject. Of course, the four guys that owned the pony did charge a fee.

Lunch couldn't come too soon, but after lunch there were more classes until midafternoon, always announced by those infernal bells, which through some auricular miracle, began to melt into the background, except for that first one in the morning. Like commercials that are attached to TV programs, it was somehow louder than all the rest.

The seminary's goal was to produce priests, men of God, who would lead the church in the decades to come. But, day to day, the faculty's challenge was just threading the needle between hoped-for holiness and human hormones. As the Good Book says (or should), "It is easier for a camel to pass through the eye of a needle than for an adolescent male to focus on God" (Matthew 9:24—not). Hence, after-school sports to keep our minds and bodies occupied, which is how we spent the several hours between classes and dinner.

It started with flag football in the fall. We only played intramural games among the other seminarians. The most popular guys would get to be the captain, and usually the quarterback. They would take turns picking the rest of the team until everybody was chosen. I was always one of the last and usually played center. If I could manage to get the ball to the quarterback and then fall down, my job was done, but it was always intimidating on the line before I snapped the ball. Even though it was "flag" or "touch" football, some of the guys who played guard were big, and there was always a chance of getting turned into roadkill.

We moved on to basketball as the year progressed. Basketball was the only sport we had even a chance of fielding a varsity team that could compete with other high schools; and even at that, I think we were in the "triple Z" league. The one school we consistently played against was the Preston School of Industry up in Ione. This was a euphemism for "reform school" and these were the bad boys. But even they felt sorry for us as they whipped our asses. "Most of us are only in for six months," one of them said, "but we hear you guys are stuck here for six years." That we were there voluntarily was beyond their ability to comprehend. The one time we managed to beat them they filed a complaint. "You guys cheated. You had a sixth man on your team today—Jesus."

And there was always the near-Olympic size swimming pool available for our use and abuse. The favorite aquatic game was "dunk the punk," a hazing activity designed to see if new students could beat Houdini's record holding their breath underwater. I had learned to swim in second grade, but Miss Lockwood had neglected to show me how to escape from three or four older boys doing their best to drown me. I didn't do much swimming at St. Pius.

They wouldn't let us have dinner until after we had prayed the rosary; fingering our beads while we said fifty "Hail Mary's," some "Our Father's," and "Glory Be's," and a few assorted other prayers thrown in for good measure. We did this while thinking about the life of Jesus and Mary, the "good, bad, and beautiful," otherwise known as the Joyful, Sorrowful, and Glorious mysteries. I never took to the rosary even though it is a staple of Catholic spirituality—too tedious and boring. The only good thing was that most days we got to pray the rosary by ourselves, outside, and while walking around.

At dinner we took turns waiting on tables and helping with the dishwashing. Every night we were supposed to get an hour or so of free time to do "anything we wanted" within the narrow confines of what the rules allowed. I often went to the high school lounge next to the refectory. The lone television set was there, but since I was a freshman with no chance of selecting the programming and wasn't used to watching TV since we didn't have one at home, I mostly amused myself with war games: newly learned chess and the world-gobbling *Risk*.

That rec room was for the high school guys. The college "men" had their own space in a separate building out by the pool hall. They had nicer furniture and a stereo to play records.

When I entered the seminary, the twelve years of priestly preparation were divided into two parts. St. Pius, where I was studying, was called a "minor seminary" and consisted of four years of high school and two years of what was then called "junior college." The second stretch of six years was the "major seminary" or Theologate, equivalent to the final two years of college and four years post-grad work in theology and pastoral training. The Theologate for the top half of California was in Menlo Park on the San Francisco Peninsula. At St. Pius, the faculty did its best to separate the "men" from the "boys," but the system in 1963 pretty much amounted to six years of high school with a few extra privileges thrown in the last couple of years.

One of the things I remember from the first few months was the time I stuck my head into the pool hall one evening. A bunch of guys were gathered around the only radio that was officially allowed on campus. Some guy named Cassius Clay was beating the crap out of another guy named Sonny Liston. From the way the guys were carrying on, I think Liston was supposed to win, but it didn't turn out that way.

11/22/63

It was a crisp November Day, about two months after school started. Late morning and we were in religion class when the knock came on the classroom door. Fr. David walked to the door and stepped out into the hallway, our signal to start chatting with one another, speculating about who might be in trouble.

He returned moments later. He spoke four words: "The president's been shot." Then the world stopped.

I could almost feel gravity losing its grip as I floated above the classroom. I looked down and saw the miniature California license plate replica taped to my desk. It was a gift from Mrs. Asbury, my mother's boss at the newspaper and our local Democratic Chairwoman. The goldenrod letters stamped a-gainst the black background spelled out JFK 464, a suddenly obsolete campaign slogan.

"We need to go to the chapel and pray," Fr. David whispered as if any such words were necessary. We stood as one. I looked across the room. Pence, the boy who tortured mice, had tears running down his cheeks. In the hall we were joined by the rest of our school. Young men, many of whom had been boys a few moments ago, silently moved towards the chapel, the only sounds our footfalls on the concrete floors and stifled sniffles.

After a few minutes of silent prayer, our rector Fr. George, whose words were always spoken with an air of gravitas, made the dreaded announcement. The hospital in Dallas had confirmed that President Kennedy was dead. Gasps. Quiet tears, some not so quiet. We prayed aloud for his soul; for his family; for our country; for ourselves. We crossed the court-yard to the refectory for a lunch no one had a stomach for. We didn't need to be cautioned to silence. Even the dishes, which normally clattered throughout the meal, fell silent, honoring the fallen leader. The news was transmitted to us in bits and pieces as more information became available.

Classes were canceled. I spent the next four days glued to the single television set in our recreation room next to the refectory. Images burned themselves into my brain. The am-bulance continuing to arrive at Parkland Hospital. Walter Cronkite tearfully announcing Kennedy's death. Jackie in her pillbox hat and bloodstained dress. Lyndon raising his right hand in the back of Air Force One. And two days later, Os-wald's smirk a moment before Ruby extinguished it. The ri-derless horse. John-John's salute.

At home, as I later learned, my mother was preparing to celebrate my youngest brother's fifth birthday when she heard the news. She collapsed onto the couch sobbing, "I always wanted him to be president, but not like this," referring to Lyndon Johnson, her former Austin, Texas, congressman, now president by bullet. My sister was only three, and she still remembers.

It was a couple of weeks later that we found out just before it was printed in the Galt newspaper, our own little quirk to this international tragedy. Our head cook at St. Pius was named Ruby (Oswald) Kennedy.

It happened just before Thanksgiving, our first time at

home since school started. What should have been a joyful reunion with our families was overshadowed by our great national tragedy. On Thanksgiving evening President Johnson spoke to the country, beginning with these words, "Tonight, on this Thanksgiving, I come before you to ask your help, to ask your strength, to ask your prayers that God may guard this Republic and guide my every labor," he began. "All of us have lived through seven days that none of us will ever forget."

He was right. Just as the attack on Pearl Harbor had marked my parent's generation and 9/11 would mark my children's, the Kennedy Assassination marked mine. And when things like this happen, it is the young who pay the highest price. *What if* Oswald's bullet had missed its mark, and certainly Sirhan's, five years later? "Vietnam War" might not be such an integral part of the American lexicon. My generation might have been free of the tragedy of war. My friend Jim, a delayed victim of Agent Orange, might still be alive. My friend Bob might still have both his legs. Fifty thousand others might have lived to father children and raise families.

But we didn't know that then. And we were protected. Men of God, even budding ones, were shielded from the horrors of war if they chose. The 4-D (divinity deferment) draft status that we would be assigned on our eighteenth birthday was far down the list from 1-A (cannon fodder).

ECCE SACERDOS

I don't know if it was the impact of the Kennedy assassination or another more direct divine action, but we began to change as the year progressed. Not much, not fast, not so anyone would really notice, but it was there.

We were still male teenagers, of course. I learned that it was not Fr. Luke but my fellow students who would pose the greatest threat to my bedmaking skills. Short sheeting, for sport or vengeance, was a common occurrence. Rare was the seminarian who never had the experience of jumping into bed just as the lights were being turned out to find that half his bed was missing, or so it seemed. One or more of his classmates had unmade his bed and re-made it with the top sheet folded in half so that his feet stopped halfway down. The victim had to either sleep with his knees in his chin all night or try to remake the bed by flashlight while the rest of us snickered.

And any new-found holiness did not prevent the almost weekly kitchen raids organized by our classmate Jordan. After lights out, and allowing a good hour or two to ensure that all of the fathers were in their rooms for the night, Jordan would sneak down to the kitchen with a flashlight, a couple of pillow-cases, and one or two assistants to steal food from the kitchen. It was hardly a haphazard event. Jordan carried shopping lists with specific requests, for which he would be compensated upon delivery. His assistants for the evening got a discount. I don't know if Jordan had obtained a kitchen key, knew how to pick locks, or had blocked the door with a bit of cardboard after getting off dish crew. I don't recall that he ever got caught, although there were several aborted missions.

Not everyone was impressed enough with what the kitchen had to offer that they would risk punishment or expulsion to participate in a kitchen raid. Someone had made this clear with his scribbling on the wall of a stall in the bathroom near the office, "Flush twice. It's a long way to the kitchen." Most of us got a chance to read his wit before Fr. Luke found it and turned its removal into a work crew assignment.

And there was the group, or groups, that took long walks down Twin Cities road to where the Consumnes River meandered through a clump of trees. Rumor has it that they lay on the grass and enjoyed the "grass." Rumor also has it that they were sometimes joined by girls from Galt High School. Since I was not part of any of these groups, my reportage is only hearsay.

Despite all these extracurriculars, and despite ourselves, all that praying and maybe even studying that damn Latin began to have an effect. Even though we had been so quickly disabused of our priestly fantasies by Fr. Luke that first day, many retained our enthusiasm for our call. We grew more cohesive as a group, although there were fewer of us to stick together. Only fifty-six of us had returned after Christmas vacation, and as the first year neared its end, just over fifty remained.

The last week of May, after finals were over, we took a class picnic. The seminary had an old two-and-a-half-ton truck someone had donated, and the brothers had restored. It was a flatbed with attached staked sides. That morning about thirty of us climbed onto the back of the truck and arranged ourselves on the hay bales that had been provided for seating. Guardian angels served as seatbelts on the drive to the "river," our destination for the day. We were headed for a swimming hole on one of the forks of the Mokelumne River. I don't know the mileage, but it took two renditions of "Ninety-nine Bottles of Beer on the Wall" and three of "The Ants Go Marching One by One" to get there. Upon arrival, we piled out, most of us already in our swimsuits or cut-offs. We noisily unloaded our picnic supplies from the truck and listened to the usual warnings about staying at the swimming hole and not venturing out into the fast-running river itself.

We hadn't been swimming too long, though, when we heard the scream. "Help, help! I can't swim." Gil, one of our classmates, had been sunning himself on a rock a little up-stream. Somehow, he had slipped into the river and was frantically trying to keep himself afloat in the fast-running water, spring melt from the snows in the Sierras.

Fr. Luke had been keeping an eye on us from the shore. Before most of us even heard Gil's cries or knew that he had fallen in, Fr. Luke was again a paratrooper from the Battle of the Bulge. Superman had nothing on him. In one smooth move, he was out of his long black cassock and into the river, the abandoned cassock floating behind him. He chased the drowning seminarian either two miles or two hundred feet—depending on who is telling the story—before he caught up with Gil and dragged him to shore like a wet rag.

The good news was that Gil was fine, and the incident was the only mishap on our whole outing.

The bad news was that Fr. Luke had blown his cover, literally and figuratively.

His fierce façade, the one that had scared me half to death on that first day the previous September, seemed to have floated down the river with his black cassock. I saw his true colors. A real man, a real man of God, who cared about his charges and was willing to risk his own life for them without thought. A priest? What was a priest? I had to ask myself that question all over again. It would take a few years, but I would like the answer I discovered.

THE CATHOLIC CHURCH
LEAVES HOME

When I returned to St. Pius as a sophomore, my world was about to change, more than I could know. By now, my class was down to fifty-two. The seven newcomers joining our class meant that eighteen of the original group had dropped out in the first year.

You wouldn't think rearranging the furniture would be that big of a deal. But it was. On Sunday, November 29th, the first Sunday of Advent and the official beginning of the Catholic Church year, the first of the major changes coming from the Second Vatican Council started being implemented. It was to be nothing short of a liturgical and theological tsunami that roared over Catholicism for the next few years.

When I came to Mass that Sunday morning, the altar had been turned around so that the priest now faced the congregation while saying the Mass.

The heavy stone altar built into the front wall of the chapel hadn't miraculously flipped itself around during the night. The Church wasn't the circus, after all, picking up and moving to a new town each day. But a new temporary altar had been set up, facing the pews, a few steps inside the altar rail. Its construction was like using an old door, set atop a couple of saw-horses, functional but hardly aesthetic. A more artistic new altar would come later and the original, now unused, would stay in place until the chapel, and the entire seminary, would be repurposed by the State of California into a training center for prison guards several years after the last seminarian had "left the building." The altars would be torn out and the immense stained-glass window would be carefully disassembled and installed in a new parish church in Sacramento. The U-shaped building would become unrecognizable for its original purpose as the prayer-place for generations of future priests that never were. Except that in some quietly negotiated church-state compromise, the first thing your eyes are drawn to upon entering through the massive front doors is the original hand-painted mural of the Savior on a three-story cross of gold, towering over several dozen cadets practicing their martial arts.

The altered altar was not a complete surprise. For a couple months we had been preparing and practicing for the new altar placement and the liturgical changes that would begin that day. Still, the experience that I joined nearly every other American Catholic that late November day represented more change than the Church had known in nearly half a millennium.

For centuries, every minute detail of what happened at Mass was dictated down to the way the priest held his fingers to pray, how many times he genuflected, and how low he bowed over the Host as he whispered the words of consecration. The minutiae were part of my faith, as if God had dictated every single movement just after kicking Adam and Eve out of the Garden of Eden.

The flipped altar wasn't the only change. Some of the prayers, which for centuries had been in Latin, apparently God's boyhood tongue, were now in English, and the congergation had to take its collective nose out of private missals and respond to what the priest was saying.

And now that the priest was looking at us, he also spoke with us. The dynamic of the service changed dramatically. Prior to this day, the priest spent the Mass time praying to God in a foreign language with his back to the congregation, who silently prayed in their pews reading missals or fingering rosary beads. A wag once noted that the comforting thing about the universality of Latin in the Roman Catholic Church was that a Catholic "could go to Mass anywhere in the world and still not understand what was going on." Now it was more of a dialogue. Shortly, temporary song sheets and then paper booklets replaced our ponderous "Libers" with English songs, originally borrowed from the Protestants before the Catholic song writers got into the act.

Not all of this happened on one single day, but that first Sunday of Advent was a dramatic beginning. And not everyone was happy about the changes. People on both sides of the altar complained that much was lost, from the deep sense of mystery to a demotion for God Himself. Fifty plus years later, some people who hadn't even been alive when the changes began still refuse to accept them.

In their fears, the naysayers understood the old Latin adage, "lex orandi, lex credendi," which literally reminded us that "how we pray determines what we believe." (See, I learned some Latin.) It took a few years, but the liturgical changes seemed to change much of what Catholics believed, how they related to Church leadership, and how they behaved.

Like every other Catholic, I was raised to believe that the Church was a top-down enterprise. God made us, and He made the rules. The original mediator, the go-between, was Jesus. And after He was transferred back to heaven, His place was taken by the clergy. The whole point of being a Catholic was to follow the rules and get to heaven. And the priest—that is, what I thought I was preparing to be—was leading the way, a step or two ahead of and above everybody else.

But when they turned those altars around and we looked at that priest in the eye and started conversing with him in a language we understood, more than prayer began to change.

The tsunami was very real and incredibly strong. Perhaps there is no better example of this than Fr. George, our seminary rector. It didn't happen the first day, but as the wave rolled on, this rock of a churchman, used to having more authority than a four-star general, literally lost his power of speech for several years, a physical manifestation of his lost spirituality.

Personally, I rode the crest of that wave like I was on a spiritual surfboard.

If Fr. Luke's orientation oration had shaken my faith in what priesthood was, then the changes emerging from Vatican II rattled the cage even more. When I first thought I wanted to be a priest, or that God was calling me, my faith was a child's, completely inherited, filtered through the adults in my life: my mother, nuns, parish priests. It was an accepting, not a questioning faith. It was the faith of everyday Catholics and even clergy of the time. I believed, like many adults do today, in speaking of the Bible, for instance, "God said it. I believe it. And that's all there is to it." I had an excuse. I was a child. The adults who believe this way today do not.

The picture I'd had of a priest was of a kind of God/man, like Jesus was said to be: one foot on earth and one in heaven. Until my own father challenged Fr. Carney over his chalice diatribe, I'd thought a priest could do no wrong. My dad showed me our pastor's feet of clay. And Fr. Luke certainly showed me that a priest could have both feet planted in the clay of the earth. Vatican II began to bring the entire church down to earth. In my high school seminary days, I didn't have all this figured out, and couldn't have articulated it this way yet, but I began absorbing it. The humanization of the Church envisioned by Pope John and the Council, sometimes despite itself, began to change me and how I saw myself as a future priest. And it was okay. More than okay.

I'd always been a good kid, not causing my parents any trouble. Now, I was a teenager, ready to get on with life, ready to make some waves of my own, looking for a cause for my rebellion. But I wasn't even at home anymore, so it was hard to rebel against my parents. Unless I got into serious trouble in the seminary that would follow me home, about the only thing my parents would ever notice that might possibly irritate them was if I grew my hair long, but that only came later. But now, the whole church was starting to act like a teenager, rebelling against its older traditional self. And I was part of that. Not just part of it, but on the cutting edge. In the seminary, even in a relative backwater like St. Pius in Galt, we *felt* the changes physically, as if they were part of puberty.

We began to read the documents emerging from Vatican II and learned that it was no longer sinful to be a Protestant. Rather than the Catholic Church being the only "true" religion, the Council Fathers proclaimed that, *while the fullness of God's presence and message might "subsist" in Catholicism, there were numerous other paths on which a person of good will could seek God with integrity.* This new approach had a name, Ecumenism. In fact, Vatican II was often referred to as the "Ecumenical Council." Front and center in this new acceptance were the Jews, so long persecuted by the Christians, whose faith ironically consisted in following a Jew, Jesus of Nazareth. This, nineteen hundred years after the crucifixion of that Jesus, but barely twenty after the liberation of Auschwitz.

Later, instead of kneeling at the altar rail with our tongues hanging out to receive the Body of the Lord, we stood, hands extended after we had first turned and greeted our neighbor with a hug or handshake and a wish for peace. Our verbal "Amen" proclaimed our agreement that the "Body of Christ" was more than the transformed Host. It was also us, the community of believers, called to be Christlike in the world.

We still prayed and did our chores and studied—including that infernal Latin, still six days a week. The church leaders might now encourage us to embrace the Jews, but they weren't ready to turn loose of Latin. Still haven't. But for us, Fr. Justin seemed more and more like an outdated set of encyclopedias. "Why should we have to continue to be tortured with this dead language?" we asked ourselves and him. He dug in, protecting his life's work and possibly his raison d'être—to use the French, which, I believe, does come from the Latin.

The bells still rang to wake us, but no longer before the cock finished crowing. Instead of our parents coming to visit us once a month for four hours, we could now go home for a weekend each month. With the completion of the new residence wing, everyone except freshmen and sophomores got at least a semi-private room.

When I had entered the seminary, just a year before, I'd joined an institution that was at the tail end of its nearly five-hundred-year history. If the Catholic Church was rigid, then the seminary system was "rigider." If the Catholic Church "had" rules, then the seminary was "made of rules." And if Vatican II unleashed a tidal wave of change in the Catholic Church, then what effect it had on the seminary system was more akin to Noah's flood.

What if the changes symbolized by turning around that altar had not happened just when they did? It's doubtful that the circus boy in me would have long remained in such a place. But my timing was good. A decade earlier, I doubt I would have stayed. And a decade later, with the closing of many seminaries, there would have been nowhere to stay.

JUST DON'T DO IT

NO. This one word, these two little letters, not only encapsulated but pretty much exhausted, the Roman Catholic Church's teaching on human sexuality as it rushed headlong into the 1960s.

I'm not referring just to what was expected of future celibates but almost everybody. It started with the Church's First Family: Joseph and Mary, not Adam and Eve. They got Jesus, without having sex. And since the Catholic Church taught that JC was an only child, they kept at it: the no sex part. Joseph spent untold hours making chairs in his carpenter shop. It's unnecessary to speculate about what Mary did since proper ladies never thought of such things.

In order to perpetuate the species, a minor exception was permitted. Couples (one male and one female only please) were permitted to "couple-u-late" under certain rigid conditions. First, they had to be married, not only legally, but also "in the Church." Then they had to have the right intention, meaning that their "getting it on" always had to be open to the production of a new "junior." Pleasure, while sometimes unavoidable in these situations, was begrudgingly acknowledged by the Church through clenched teeth, but it had to be entirely secondary.

At least you could think about it. Well, NO. We finally found out what Sister meant when she had us include the unspecified "bad thoughts" in our second-grade confessions. As our otherwise moral thirty-ninth president Jimmy Carter would later acknowledge, even "lusting in one's heart" fell into the NO category. And he isn't even Catholic.

How about leaving everybody else alone and just taking care of yourself? Again NO. Masturbation, a.k.a. "self-abuse," was about the biggest sin an adolescent, seminarian or otherwise, could commit. And we're not talking about your everyday venial sin here, even though for many it was at least a daily occurrence. If you wanked your weenie and didn't get to confession before one of your classmates drowned you in the swimming pool or something, you'd go straight to H-E-L-L. There was an unmarked, but very real, line from the Playboy magazine hidden under your mattress to the confessional box, where one of the seminary's dozen or so priests was always ready to hear you confess your indiscretion.

How did I learn about all this? From God's golden record. Once a year, Fr. David, our religion teacher, would pull out His "golden record" (the LP really was a translucent gold color) and set it to spin on a portable record player while he absented himself from the classroom for the twenty minutes or so it took to play.

Time has dimmed my memory of many of the specifics of the golden record. If the record held any record at all, it was probably for misconceptions and inaccurate information. As teenage boys, we all acted much better informed about the birds and the bees than we actually were. But even we could have taught that gold record a thing or two.

It was mostly about what we weren't supposed to do, or what we were supposed to do to avoid the things we weren't supposed to do. We'd all so given up on avoiding masturbation that none of the record's advice, which probably included tidbits such as praying the rosary—fingering the beads instead of ourselves—or taking a cold shower would have even registered. The record probably went on to note the convoluted theological reasons why God, who had provided us with the equipment, forbade its use. Our concerns were more practical. If we had any fears, they focused less on the likelihood of going to hell than getting caught in the act or going blind, as an old wives' tale warned.

If there was a silver lining in any of this, it was the Catholic belief in confession. Wank your weenie; fess up; go to Holy Communion. Repeat as necessary.

And that was it. Theoretically, I guess, listening to that record prepared us, not only to remain chaste ourselves but to counsel our parishioners after ordination. And while we were listening to the golden record, not a hundred miles away, half the guys in our generation—the ones not getting blown to bits in 'Nam—were screwing their brains out with hippie chicks in San Francisco.

The facts are that God came up with hormones before He got around to starting religion. Ain't no way you're going to stop sex. We seminarians were a strange mixture of interests and desires. We were where we were because we wanted to serve God, not a typical situation for an adolescent male. Certainly, motives were mixed. Some guys were pushed into it by family, usually mothers, and some just wanted to get away from an unpleasant home. And none of us were anywhere near mature enough to know what we were getting into or to make the decision we thought we were making. But there was still something special about us. In some inchoate way, we were reaching beyond ourselves, searching for greater meaning than that sold by American media and teen culture. Fifty years later, when I encounter some of my former classmates, a bit of that spark is still there. Something set us apart. Then and now. We may not have saved the world for God or from itself, but we each tried in some small way: lives lived not just for ourselves but for others. But that didn't mean we didn't have eyes, ears, and, well... other stuff.

I always liked girls, ever since I'd put my arms around Tommy's waist as she pedaled us down the street on my new tricycle. But for most of my high school career it was entirely academic. Before I sprouted, I could have been the only guy in a room full of young women my age, and they still wouldn't have noticed me unless they were looking for their little brother. I have a photo of me and an attractive young woman, a head taller, on prom night. It was taken by my mother. The photo is deceiving. Being in the seminary, it certainly wasn't my prom. Mother was trying to expand her photo business by selling high school prom photos. I had gone along as an assistant, and she had used me and this young lady as models as she adjusted her camera settings and lighting. It was probably the closest I got to participating in a normal high school social event.

I think most of the guys in the seminary shared my interest in the other half of the species. There may have been some of us who entered for the express purpose of avoiding the opposite sex, but most had the normal adolescent male feelings in this department. We may have been shy or socially inept but mostly just didn't have much opportunity. We knew what the vow of celibacy involved and had theoretically pledged ourselves to it, but it wasn't real, not yet anyway. Or we thought we would fool around as long as we could. The point is that most of us were run-of-the-mill heterosexual teenage males.

Not all of course. Due to its obvious peculiarities, the Catholic priesthood probably attracts more than the average population of gay candidates: no expectation to marry a woman, focus on the more spiritual or aesthetic dimensions of one's personality, and proximity to other such males in a closed environment. But despite spending eight years in Catholic seminaries, I am a complete non-expert on gay men in the seminary or priesthood. It's like I drove through those eight years with blinders on. I was just too busy with my studies, my own small group of friends, and working to pay my way through seminary to notice some of the extracurricular activity that was going on around me. In high school the one guy who was openly gay—although that term was not yet in common use—was my roommate one semester, after we got semi-private rooms as juniors. I do recall that one evening, returning from his shower clad only in his towel, he remarked how stimulating a hot shower was before bedtime. If it was an invitation, it went right on past me. Usually "gayness," which was officially prohibited, would come to light through whispered rumor, as one or more students were unceremoniously expelled in the middle of the night.

LITTLE BILL

Me? I was more than a bit naïve. I just wasn't that tuned into what was going on around me, sexually speaking. I was a "late bloomer," and I had my own set of problems.

Some things have a way of sticking with you, even if you don't want them to. I remember this like yesterday over half a century ago.

The room was spare, furnished only as necessary. It was cool, edging towards uncomfortable, and I was sitting on a table, its paper cover clinging to my bare ass, my boxer shorts bunched around my ankles.

His hands had been on my genitals, gripping, prodding, pushing. Now he's talking calmly, quietly, but I'm not reassured. Just the opposite. My insides are getting as cold as my bare bottom. I hear fragments of words like "unusual," "late," "small," "underdeveloped," but he's not talking to me.

So, I'm sitting there on the cold exam table, naked where it counts, a pre-pubescent teenager, and this doctor, who skipped sensitivity class in medical school, is discussing the lack of appropriate physical maturity with my mommy. It was like I wasn't even there, like I was some science experiment gone awry. Neither the doctor nor my mother talked to me about what was going on with me. Not then. Not ever. Ditto for me. I never spoke about my feelings, the insecurity, the doubts this interaction caused me. Not ever.

I avoided doctors throughout my teen years and don't recall finding myself standing nude before a medical person again until I followed the red line into the exam room at the Oakland Induction Center where I had been invited by my local draft board. They grabbed me by the balls and had me cough, which somehow helped them discern that I could serve as cannon fodder for Mr. Nixon's ego.

Up until that moment in the doctor's office, I don't think I had given a thought to my own sexuality, at least not in a genital way. Throughout my grade school career, I was always the shortest person in my class—not just the shortest boy, the shortest *person*. Even little Rosemary who headed the girl's line when we prepared to go back to class after recess seemed at least a touch taller, although I suppose that could have been the way she poofed her hair.

But now, that day, right in the doctor's office, my self-esteem about my maleness, which I hadn't previously been conscious of, took a long dive off a short pier. It was a deep dive, one that took years to surface from, assuming I have.

I grew up a little late but otherwise normal. The summer after my sophomore year, I must have shot up a good six inches, but it took a lot longer than that for my head to clear. I'm fortunate in that in other areas—my self-confidence has always been strong—to make up. I can handle myself well around an IQ test, and I think my birth order and unusual name gave me a fairly healthy sense of self. Still, the scar from that long-ago doctor visit stays with me.

I was at the doctor's to get my physical exam so that I could enter the seminary.

At St. Pius we slept in dorms, a dozen or so boys to a room, with a communal shower room between every two dorms.

The showers were large tiled rooms where six or eight guys could clean up at once. We were only allowed in the dorms at night, so showers were before bed or after rising—no way to escape. Normally you could wrap a towel around your waist going to and from the shower; and, if you were lucky, you could get one of the corner shower heads, thus minimizing exposure. But often you got stuck smack dab in the center, like the middle coach seat in a long airplane ride. Full Monty.

It turns out, size does matter, if not to women (I can't speak for them), at least to other developing young men. And, of course, there was a pecking—or pecker—order. Like Peter's peck of peppers, everybody sneaked a peek at other people's peters/peckers. The more advanced guys, the ones who had started puberty while they were still teething, were mostly nonchalant about matters. But not Little Bill. He was about an inch taller and six months ahead of me in the body hair department. Out of sadism, or self-protection, he made it his job in life to ensure that I knew I was lower on the sexual totem pole than he was.

"Cherub" is what he called me, like cupid and the other pudgy, hairless angels. But it got worse. When he would see me heading for a shower, he would often sneak in and steal my towel hanging from the hooks. Then he would plant himself front and center as I had to walk that gauntlet of beds down the dorm, buck naked and dripping wet. If he could manage to stick his leg out and trip me, so much the better. On particularly festive nights, this could be combined with other guys snapping their towels at you when you were down. It hurt in more ways than one.

Now I'm not a violent man and don't own a gun. But if I ever run across Little Bill again, I'd have no problem using him for target practice. It's probably a little late for the good doctor. I'm sure he and his medical degree are already rotting in the ground somewhere.

***

I suppose that no discussion of sex and priesthood is complete without facing the elephant in the room: sexual predators. I was an altar boy and a seminarian and until halfway through high school was cherubic and hairless, a likely candidate for abuse. I rubbed shoulders with dozens of priests, and nuns, in my childhood and adolescence. But as far as I can recollect, none of the clergy acted in the least way inappropriately towards me or anyone I personally knew in grade school or either of the seminaries I attended.

That doesn't mean I didn't come close.

Not one hundred feet from my bed in the dorm my freshman year when Little Bill was bullying me, was the bedroom suite of Fr. Robert. Most of the priests and brothers lived in a separate wing of the seminary just past the chapel. But each floor of each student dorm wing provided a suite, including office, study, and bedroom for a priest who served as dorm monitor. Among their duties was to make sure that everyone was in bed on time for lights out. I don't know if there was any official protocol for bed checks, but Fr. Robert had his own system. He would begin in one dorm on one side of the building, walk slowly through the shower room which connected the dorms, cross the hall, and reverse the process on the other side in order to get back to his own suite.

It seemed to serve a legitimate purpose, but even in freshman year, there were rumors that Fr. Robert, known as Bogota Bob because of his missionary service in Columbia, might seem to linger just a bit too long in the shower rooms. A friend of mine remembers that Bogota Bob would often return, sometime after lights out, ostensibly to ensure that guys were focusing on sleeping and not masturbating.

Like many Catholics, I learned about the extent of this problem in the church after the fact, including some real horror stories in other seminaries and similar institutions.

When the list of known, or reasonably likely abusers was released by the Archdiocese of Seattle, where I later worked as an adult, no fewer than seven people I personally knew and another dozen I knew of, made the list: two pastors I'd worked for; one I'd refused to work with for other reasons; two who were pastors of parishes in which I lived; and even one who was a colleague and friend. The only woman on the list was my children's grade school principal.

Curious, I checked the records of some of the other dioceses I had lived in while growing up and going to the seminary. I found Bogota Bob. His "resume" showed that he had served at St. Pius from 1959 to 1967. My freshman year of 1963 was smack dab in the middle of his time there. He later served in two regular parishes in the Sacramento diocese until he was suddenly "retired" in 1986 and transferred to his religious order's headquarters back in Wisconsin.

The reason? In that same year, 1986, he had been reported for abusing a seminarian in 1962, the year before he did my dorm check every evening. The abuse likely happened in his suite at the end of my dorm hallway. But the cryptic report simply stated: date range of alleged abuse, 1962. Male, under the age of 18. Nature of accusation(s): sexual touching and fondling. Year reported to diocese: 1986.

Given the church's reluctance to "out" the abusers, I could find no other information. But considering how quickly the diocese moved him away it's unlikely the situation was limited to one occurrence with one boy.

And I had one more "close encounter of the abuser kind" before I left St. Pius. In my last year there we were encouraged to help out in local Catholic parishes, usually teaching catechism classes to grade-schoolers. My assignment was St. Anne's in the nearby town of Lodi.

While nothing untoward happened in the parish during the year I was there, a few years afterwards a young cleric from Ireland was stationed in the parish. Remember "Merlin the Magician," the bishop who had confirmed me when I was in seventh grade at Holy Spirit school in Fairfield? He was now the bishop of the Stockton diocese in which St. Anne's was located. That meant that he was that new priest's boss; and it was at St. Anne's that the Rev. Oliver O'Grady turned on his charm and began his reign of terror, victimizing both young girls and boys as well as their mothers who had been placed in his "spiritual" charge.

Neither Merlin nor his successor did anything to O'Grady other than move him from parish to parish throughout the diocese. It took several years and the efforts of a Calaveras County sheriff's deputy to bring him to at least partial justice. And, as fate would have it, that deputy was a friend of one of my brothers who had also attended St. Pius. Later on, I learned that one of O'Grady's victims had been a young woman from my hometown, Fairfield, and had attended the same grade school where Merlin had confirmed me some years before. Fortunately, I never had the "pleasure" of meeting Ollie O'Grady, but these near encounters were creepy enough. I felt for the victims and thought again of how easily I could have been a victim myself of someone like O'Grady. *What if?*

***

There are bad individuals in every walk of life. And, I think, even more regrettable, average people can sometimes do bad things. Every act of abuse hurts the victim, and the ripples spread to their family, friends, and community. But we can deal with this. Perpetrators can be brought to justice; people can heal; forgiveness can be granted; sometimes even rehabilitation can occur (although apparently not in the case of Oliver O'Grady).

But the much larger sin lies in the corporate cover-up: denials and moving abusers around to place other victims in harm's way.

And it goes deeper: a fatal systemic flaw that is exemplified in the case of my colleague, and friend, who was eventually exposed as an abuser. Let's call him Dan. He died a few years ago but still has family around.

I knew him to be a person who was genuinely concerned about others, was a good priest and tried to make the world a better place, as far as I could see. When the cover-ups were beginning to fall apart in the 1980s and '90s, he acknowledged that he had, essentially, fondled a number of teenage boys during a church-sponsored summer camp a decade or so before. He claimed it had only happened a few times; he believed that he was providing "backrubs" so his charges could settle in for the night.

He only went so far as to admit to touching their buttocks. Maybe that's as far as he went. Maybe his psyche couldn't admit more. Perhaps he was some horrible monster whose activities went far beyond and for much longer than he acknowledged, and he fooled us all. But I think not.

The young men he abused suffered, even if it was a single event. Their lives were changed, and they carried the burden for many years. It was wrong, and when the church eventually "defrocked" him, it was the right thing to do.

Having gone through the seminary system only a few years behind Dan, it's no great stretch for me to imagine that his psycho-social development was not far removed at thirty from that of the teenagers he molested. In some way of viewing it, he may have been "acting out," exploring his own adolescent sexuality.

The system set people up. What can you expect when you sequester developing adolescents in a cloistered environment? What chance do they have to develop normally regarding their sexuality, whether it be straight or gay?

They've changed the system, somewhat, a little tinkering. Boys no longer enter the seminary in high school, or, for the most part, even college. They seek older men now, more experienced, supposedly more familiar with the complexities of life. Seminaries include psychological evaluation and counseling. But it raises even more questions. The newer batches of priests seem more conservative, less understanding of their increasingly diverse congregations.

And it's still not enough. Still not enough native celibates are coming out of American seminaries to fill the need, which is increasingly being filled with foreign priests—Nigerians, Filipinos, Vietnamese—countries where priestly ordination is still a passport to a better life in America. Good men, for the most part, but unfamiliar with the culture, the customs, the language of the people they are sent to serve. And, increasingly, contemporary cases of abuse are including more of these men. It's a bit like the tobacco industry: losing market share in the U.S., shipping their carcinogens overseas to the "less developed" world.

All this so they can keep a guy from getting married.

PART III

IT'S CARNIVAL TIME

THE FIXER

After Uncle Franco's ex-wife repossessed the elephants and took them to a circus back East, the Richards family's three-generation run as circus owners was finally over.

It was time to join the carnival.

Carnivals and circuses are not the same, but they are. Circuses feature tents and performers. Carnivals have games of chance and merry-go-rounds. But, as the American traveling circus began to experience its nadir in the early part of the twentieth century, carnivals began their ascendancy following the introduction of the Ferris Wheel at the "White City," Chicago's 1883 World's Fair. My family, like many other circus families, turned to the carnival to earn a livelihood.

By the time I was finishing my second year of seminary studies, Uncle Rusty had landed a job as booking agent and advance man with a small carnival owned by a young couple. It was the not very creatively named Carnival Time Shows, as if someone had been trying to think of an exciting name for their new enterprise and had just given up.

The show had a blank in its schedule in mid-June, and my mother helped my uncle secure a location just outside the gates of Travis Air Force Base where my dad worked, a few miles from our home in Fairfield. In return, the carnival owners agreed to offer me a summer job as a ticket seller.

The job requirements were having a good bladder—due to needing to sit in a small, cage-like ticket box for hours at a time—and being able to count. At that point in my career, my bladder was young and elastic, and I could count. I could count really well and really fast. It would take a few weeks for the carnival owners to realize what a bargain they were getting for the dollar an hour they were paying me, a quarter less than the required California minimum wage at the time. When things got busy, I could outperform any two other ticket sellers combined, particularly at the fairs when tickets were pegged at odd prices like thirty-five cents, and customers stood in line to buy them in groups of five, ten, and twenty. Our only equipment was a tin cash box, as hand calculators hadn't yet been invented.

That first Wednesday afternoon started out slow; people still at work and kids in school. At about 3:30 I noticed a young man walking around the nearly empty carnival lot, looking at the rides, kicking up small clouds of dirt with his (originally) white, high-top tennis shoes. The third time around, he stopped at the window of my ticket booth. "Mister," he said, "Can you gimme some tickets so I can ride the rides?" I looked through the screened window of the booth at a black lad of nine or ten, probably just out of class for the day.

"I'm sorry," I said, "but the tickets aren't mine. They belong to the carnival owners."

"Oh, come on man, just a couple. They won't never know."

"I'm afraid they will. They're all numbered, and then I'll have to pay for them. It'll come out of my salary."

His face contorted, and his expression immediately changed. He glared at me with a hateful scowl hundreds of years older than he was and blurted out, "White nigger! You nuthin' but a white nigger!" and stormed off.

I sat there stunned, my open mouth catching flies. A week earlier, I'd been finishing up my second year of seminary, being holy, studying about God and Jesus, and now, half a day a carnie, I was already being called the worst thing that little kid could think of.

I never saw that young man again, but I've wondered what became of him many times over the last half-century. It was June of 1965, less than a year after Lyndon Johnson, a son of the South, had signed the Civil Rights Act. The Act was the result, in part, of the bravery of the Freedom Riders of the previous decade. Some of them, the Caucasians who had joined their black brothers and sisters in the struggle were derided as "white niggers," but I don't think that's what my accuser had in mind.

When I first discovered that I was a "circus boy" visiting my Uncle Franco's circus in Wisconsin, it was, as they say, "all good." Being from a circus background was special. It made me unique. I wore it as a badge of honor. But now, starting with that black lad at my ticket window, I began to see the other side. Circus people, and carnies, were looked down on, regarded as something less than desirable human beings, even by those historically on the bottom rungs. Half a century later it still holds true. "Carnie" carries a lot of negative baggage, and I don't think I've ever heard the term used positively. And the circus? "It's a real circus," they say when things are a total mess of confusion, apparently not knowing that the U.S. Army, preparing for war, once sought advice from the Ringling Circus, acknowledged experts on the logistics involved in moving a city of fifteen hundred humans and animals overnight on a mile-long train.

Circus bad, church good. That was the prevailing wisdom, but I didn't buy it. I just figured that God had gotten Himself a better PR department since the Inquisition.

When I walked up to the office window on Wednesday of my second week on the carnival, one of the owners JoAnne

Davis said, "Engineer, go see 'Speed.' He's the guy with the receding gray hair over by the light plant [power generator]. He'll find you something to do, as we don't have enough ticket seller jobs this week." The show was set up in the parking lot of a small strip mall in Santa Rosa. It was a true "still spot" meaning that there was no festival or celebration; the carnival erected fewer rides and games and hoped there would be enough business just to cover expenses.

As I later learned, the ticket-selling jobs were usually held by young women referred to as "Possum Belly Annies." They were the live-in girlfriends, however temporary, of the ride boys. The name came from the storage spaces under the semi-trucks, known as "possum bellies." Over the road these spaces carried electrical wire, tools, and miscellaneous ride parts. But once the carnival was set up, they provided a boudoir for the ride boys and their girlfriends. (On most modern carnivals, the show provides trailered bunkhouses for the help: a safer, cleaner, and somewhat more private environment. But in the mid-sixties, when other young people were sleeping in communal settings in San Francisco and elsewhere, no one gave it much thought).

"Speed" was the carnival's ride foreman, responsible for setting up the rides and supervising the operators—"ride boys," as they were called. He got his nickname because on Sunday nights he handed out the little white pills that helped those ride boys negotiate the trucks to the next spot after they had operated rides for eight or ten hours and then spent another six tearing them down and loading them on the trucks.

I found Speed, introduced myself, and told him what JoAnne had said. A man of few words, he motioned me to follow him to Kiddieland. My new job was to be the operator of a kiddie ride: the fish ride. This thrill-a-minute device for the under-five set consisted of eight fish-shaped cars, each painted a different bright color and each holding one victim in its rounded belly. The fish went in a circle on a metal track, and the track was built on a wave pattern, so the children rose up and down in their little fishy as they went round and round, like a whale on the ocean.

"Okay, Engineer, this is where you'll be working this week. Keep this gate shut. Let the little kids in one at a time after you take a ticket from their parents. They usually want to pick out their own color of fish to ride in. Lift them up; put them on the seat; and be sure, absolutely sure, to fasten the belt around their waist. Be *sure*.

"Over here is the control box. After you have loaded all the kids, close the gate again and come over here. Tear up the tickets and put them through the slot in the wooden box next to the control. Now you raise the handle to start the ride and pull it back down to stop it a few minutes later. Do you have a watch? The ride is supposed to last three minutes. Most of the bigger rides have timers but this one is old-fashioned. After the ride's over, undo the belts, and let the kids go back to their folks.

"That's about all there is to it. Every couple of hours, if we're not jammed up, either me or my assistant Chico will come and give you a break. Got it? Any questions?"

"No, sir. I think I understand," I said.

At first it was fun, kinda, although after a while I wished I had my ticket selling job back. After dark it got cold, and I had forgotten my jacket. A couple hours in, I did something wrong. I don't know if I forgot to strap a kid in, if she undid the strap herself, or the ride stopped too abruptly when I flipped the switch to stop, but suddenly one of the fish disgorged its little Jonah unto the pavement amid screams and yells from the parents.

I froze as the little girl's dad pushed the fence and me aside and rushed to grab his sobbing daughter. Probably before I could even remember my own name, Speed and a couple of other carnies were there, talking with the parents, and getting the other kids off the ride.

After some of the commotion had died down and we knew that the little girl was going to be okay, Speed told me he was going over to the office to talk with JoAnne. Since I had failed at a kiddie ride, I was hardly in line to operate the Ferris wheel and was sent home for the night. I was sure I'd be fired, my carnival career lasting just over a week.

But I didn't get fired, and the next week I had my ticket-selling job back.

A slight, weather-worn man in a houndstooth jacket walked up to the side of my ticket box.

"You must be Engineer the priest," he said.

"I'm not really a priest yet, just studying to be one," I replied.

"I'm Jack, Jack Kent. I saw what happened last week on the fish ride. Sorry about that, but don't worry yourself. The little girl wasn't hurt. I think she unbuckled the seat belt while the ride was going, but who knows. Anyway, I took care of it. Only cost the show a cotton candy, couple of corn dogs, and a few ride tickets."

"Well, thanks. They sent me home right away. Didn't know if I'd still have a job."

"This is a carnival. It takes a lot more than that to get bounced around here."

"Those your walks?" Jack asked, referring to the handful of nickels and dimes on the counter to the left of the slot where the money came in and the tickets went out.

"Walks? What do you mean?" I asked. "That's some change a couple of people forgot to take. I yelled at them, but they must have been in a hurry to get on a ride."

"Well, mister-almost-a-priest, I heard you were from a circus family, but you're a real 'first of May,' aren't you?"

"What's a 'first of May'?"

"That's carnie for a newbie, a greenhorn, somebody who just joined the show. They generally start at the beginning of a season, around the first of May."

"Let me help you a little bit with your carnie education," Jack went on. "Short-changing customers, now that's something that will get you fired, at least if you get caught. Used to be a lot more common on carnivals, circuses too. But it caused too many 'beefs,' burned out, too many 'spots' that the show couldn't play again, even a couple of years later. 'Walks' are a little different. People get excited. Leave their change. End of the day, it's yours. But you're smart to leave it sitting on the counter like that, at least for a little while. That way, if they come back, you can hand it right back to them. Makes 'em think you're honest. Good thing for the show."

"You mean I don't have to turn that money into the office at the end of the night?" I asked.

"Shit, no. Oh, sorry. Didn't mean to offend. Never turn in more money than you've sold tickets for. It's yours. Kind of a 'fringe benefit,' you could say. That little bit doesn't look like much now but, trust me, it'll pile up. You'll find ways to 'help' it get bigger. By the way, I collect liberty dimes, the ones we had before the Roosevelts started being minted. Keep an eye out and save 'em for me. I'll come around at the end of the night and buy 'em off you." This didn't come across as a request, but as a statement from a man who didn't have to say please.

Jack was the show's "fixer" or "patch." He didn't fix rides or electrical wiring. He fixed people, like the parents of the little girl who fell off the fish ride. He patched up "beefs" when a guy griped because he lost too much money at one of the games and threatened to go to the police.

And every week he had to fix the cops. Sometimes it was just a handful of tickets for their kids. Usually it was scheduling enough "off-duty" police for extra security. It was surprising how many extra cops were needed, even for a small carnival. Or Jack was bailing ride guys out of jail so they could drive the trucks to the next spot. Carnivals have a well-deserved reputation for a little larceny; at least that was the case half a century ago. Now, on their worst day, they didn't even begin to compare to your average politician, lawyer, or corporation. But the carnies got the bad rep.

Jack didn't go to school to become a carnival fixer unless you count the school of hard knocks. He was the show "patch" because of his other business. Jack also owned the "flat stores" on the show. It was the flat stores that generated most of the serious beefs and required the most fixing. It was the flat stores, that put a lot of money in Jack's pockets, and, next to the rides, put the most in the carnival owner's for his share. And it was the flat store revenues that helped keep the entire show afloat in the muddy lots during "poor time": the rainy weeks in spring when the show first emerged from its winter quarters.

Aside from the rides, most of the other profit centers on the carnival are called "joints." The burger stand is the "grab" joint." The souvenir stand is known as the "garbage joint." The games—the rest of the joints—were erected each week out of sticks and canvass. Except for the glass pitch, nearly all of them gave out "plush" (stuffed animals), as prizes. A couple of exceptions were the "prize every time" games over in Kiddie-land. Everybody who played won and the prize was "slum," little trinkets that cost the game operator as little as a penny and guaranteed that he also won every time on even a ten-cent play. It kept the little kids happy.

But the flat stores were different. Jack's two joints were housed in gleaming silver Airstream trailers, and when their fronts opened, they displayed a dazzling array of merchandise that drew the guys, especially the macho men, like an electro-magnet. He had bicycles, color televisions, power tools, and shotguns, all basking under glaring white neon lights and almost calling out to those guys, *"Come on big fella, take me home."* This was a step beyond winning a stuffed animal for your girl. This was big-game safari time. Send the kids off to the rides with the wife. A man needs to focus. It was no accident that the basic game set-up resembled a football game.

"Hey, buddy, come on over here. I got a free game for ya." Won't cost ya a dime. Look at this stuff we're givin' away. Don't make me take it to the next town."

"Uh, okay. How do I play?"

"You a football fan? Sure, you are. Well, you already know the rules then. All ya gotta do is get to the goal post. Here, let me show you. This one's on me."

The "mark" (customer) stepped a little closer.

"Normally, you start in your own end zone, here"—he pointed to the board on the counter, "but this afternoon I'm gonna start you on the twenty-yard line. Here, throw the dice in this cup."

The mark would throw the dice. "Thirty-four. That puts you over the fifty on the first throw. You musta been a quarterback in high school. So, you wanna win something? Starts at two bucks a throw?"

"Yeah, I guess."

"Well, first let's decide what you're playing for. How about a clock radio or one of those electric drills?"

"Is that a twelve-gauge up there?'

"This baby? Sure is. Have a closer look at her."

He examines the shotgun. "That's what I want."

"You got good taste. The shotgun's our most valuable item today. But it cost five bucks a roll to play for the gun. That okay with you?"

After two more rolls the guy would be inside the five-yard line. On his fourth roll the "flattie" would tell him, "Sorry buddy. Too many yards this time. Puts you out of the end zone. And that was your fourth down. But here's the thing about this game. The other team never gets to play. So, you can keep going with a new set of downs. But since you're so close, inside the five, it's ten dollars a down."

Fifteen minutes later, the "flattie" might have taken the guy for nearly a "yard" (one hundred dollars), and he still wouldn't have managed to get into the end zone. Feeling that he was reaching the guy's limit, the game operator would send him off with a cheap knock-off "Rolex".

In a way, the flat stores were the "surest" thing on the midway. You were guaranteed to lose. There was no way to win, no matter how much you spent trying. Jack's "agents," the guys who operated the game, looked nothing like the rest of the carnies—used car salesman, perhaps, but not carnies. In another life, they could have just as well have been hedge fund managers.

Walks. I pondered the term and the reality. It made sense. It was an all-cash, fast-paced, business. People got excited. Kids wanted on the rides. Parents didn't want to listen to their screaming if they had to wait in line an extra turn. And the google-eyed teenage boys could almost feel their girl's budding boobies squished up against them on the Scrambler as it flung them around with its centrifugal force. It should be no mystery why carnival rides are so popular with teenage males. So, I could understand how people could occasionally forget their change in their excitement.

And what could I do? I was trapped in a four-foot square plywood ticket box, not entirely unlike that confessional booth of my first confession. And instead of sins, I had the carnival's money and rolls of tickets, which were even better than money. I couldn't very well run out and chase someone down the midway to return their change, especially not with a line of people waiting to buy tickets. But what about Jack's comments about "helping" the walks grow? That was a mystery, but one that I would soon solve, for better or worse.

Even before God invented Catholics, He'd come up with the Ten Commandments. The nuns in grade school had skipped over the ones about "adultery" and "coveting another man's wife"; and murder didn't seem like an immediate concern to grade-schoolers. The most I remembered about that one was that the Catholic Church's "Just War" theory meant that God granted an exception if a guy was wearing the wrong color uniform. But the two commandments about lying and stealing got a lot of play in our daily religion class. If we wanted a shot at heaven, or even just purgatory, we needed to tell the truth, even if it hurt, and not take anything that didn't belong to us. And I'd certainly had my struggles over the "biggie" of missing Mass on Sundays.

The sisters had acted as though God's rules were clear and rigid, almost as if they had come directly from His mouth to their ears before they pounded them into ours. But now, faced with some of life's harsher economic realities, things were becoming a bit fuzzier.

After I knew I had gotten the job on the carnival, but before I went to work, I realized that the job would involve working on Sundays, *a.k.a. the Lord's Day.* I reasoned that if you couldn't haul your ass out of a hole on the Sabbath (Matthew 14:5), then it would sure be a sin of some kind to sell tickets to carnival rides. I went to one of our parish priests to explain my dilemma.

"Father, my dad told me that after two years in the seminary, I'd have to come up with my own tuition if I wanted to continue. With several other kids in school here at Holy Spirit, he just doesn't have the extra money. So, I got a summer job."

"Well, that's good, son. You're doing the right thing, following God's call, and honoring your father and mother." Which, of course, was another one of the esteemed commandments.

"I know, Father, but the job I got is on a carnival."

"It's okay to work on a carnival. God loves all his children. Just remember that you're a Catholic, and a seminarian besides, so be sure to avoid occasions of sin."

"I will, Father, but my problem is that the carnival is open on Sunday, and to keep the job, I have to work on the Lord's Day."

The priest was silent. "Hmm," was all he said for a minute

or so. "Hmm."

"Well, son, under the circumstances, I think you should take the job. If God wants you to be a priest and he hasn't provided your family with the wealth to pay your way, then maybe this is His way of helping out."

I didn't realize it that day, but that faint sound I'd heard was little pieces of my religious armor beginning to sluff off onto the pavement. God had His rules, but there were exceptions. I guess I shouldn't have been too surprised, the advice I was getting was coming from a guy who worked mainly one day a week, and that was always a Sunday.

And off I went, never looking back at this theological conundrum again.

Another chink in my blind faith.

So, a few weeks later, I found myself sitting in my ticket box pondering Jack Kent's words about "helping" my "walks." It was later that day, or perhaps the next, that a guy came up with his wife and several kids and ordered a lot of tickets, the thirty-five centers for the regular rides, and some quarter kiddie-ride ones. "That'll be five dollars and eighty cents, Sir," I said as I tore the tickets from the roll. As I was handing him the tickets, he pushed a ten-dollar bill through the half-moon slot of the ticket box. Just as he did, a gust of wind came through and blew the ten onto the floor. I got off my stool and reached down to the floor to retrieve it. When I stood back up, the guy, his family, and his tickets were nowhere to be seen, and the next customer was already ordering her tickets. I expected that the man would return shortly to claim his change. But he didn't.

I put the ten under my cash box and continued selling until my line was gone. Then, to make sure I wasn't dreaming, forgetting, or had made a mistake, I counted all my money and balanced it against the number of tickets I had sold. I was over, four dollars plus, nearly half a day's pay. The guy had walked off leaving four dollars in change. Remembering what Jack had said I placed four one-dollar bills under the small stack of coins on the counter to the left of the half-moon slot.

I don't know, or don't want to admit, whether the practice, the plan, or the justification came first, but before long, I had developed my own "walk-building" routine. The first thing was to take the money, especially if it were a larger bill. Set it on the inside lid of the cash box out of the customer's sight. Get the customer's ticket order and count off the tickets and hand them to her. Talk to her a few seconds about how fun the rides were, how cute her kids were; it didn't matter what. Then, and only then, get the coin change from the box and push it out the half-moon-shaped slot, preferably parking it in the "blind spot" on the counter. Finally, go back to the money box and get any currency change the customer had coming. Do all this as slowly as practicable, depending on the size of the line.

I almost convinced myself that this was okay with God. I was already too theologically sophisticated to believe that the breeze that blew the ten-dollar bill onto the floor was the breath of God, but still, I needed to make five hundred dollars over the summer to pay my seminary tuition in the fall. Even with the fifty-plus hour weeks we sometimes worked, I calculated that I was still going to come up short at the dollar an hour the carnival was paying me. If, as the priest said, God would understand my dishonoring His day to pay my tuition, then certainly He wouldn't mind me helping myself to make a few more bucks with walks. I never actually shortchanged anyone and always kept the money handy to immediately return it if they came back, which they occasionally did.

LE CIRQUE REDUX

Before long, my same-age cousin Bonnie, who we called LBJ so as not to confuse her with my aunt Bonnie, had joined me as a ticket seller. Besides our math skills, the carnival owners knew that we would not "re-hash." This was another way the "help" enhanced their meager salaries—and was why the ride boys and the possum-belly girls had so jealously guarded the ticket selling jobs. The ticket sellers sold the tickets, all of which were numbered, so they couldn't cheat that way. Their ride-operator boyfriend was supposed to take a numbered ticket from each rider, tear it in half, and put it in a box by the ride. But everyone knew that the office never tried to put the torn tickets back together and count them. Even if they could, it was still impossible to tell which ride tickets came from which ticket box. So, the ride boys would palm a few tickets now and then and hand them back to their girlfriend ticket seller, who would then re-sell them to customers and pocket the money. This is one of the reasons that Jack Kent had told me to be sure not to turn in too much money. Doing so could make it look like I was "re-hashing."

Even with just Bonnie and I working, the carnival owners

noticed the difference in their revenue. Although we competed ferociously with one another to see who could "make" the most walks, we never considered cheating our employers. Since most of the other carnies knew that our family was friends with the carnival owners, none ever asked any of us to join them in a re-hash scheme. Even though we were kids, we became valued employees, especially during the busy fair season, when we probably saved the owners several thousand dollars a year.

By mid-summer, my job had become a family affair. Mother had five sons and a daughter; and my aunt, her sister, had an almost corresponding set of three daughters and a son. My mother had raised her younger sister, so the families were quite close. For Mother, it was the circus all over again. We got to travel, camp out on the fairgrounds, and be in the middle of the action. We ate fair food, and in the mornings, or sometimes, late at night after the fair closed, we'd go into town and eat something approaching regular food at the local diner.

The "candy wagon" was a sixteen-foot trailer that served cotton candy, snow cones, popcorn, caramel apples, and corn dogs: the five food groups of carnival life. In the carnival world it traditionally belonged to the owner's wife, in this case Jo-Anne Davis. She needed girls—no males please—to spin cotton candy, dip corn dogs, and make sales. My aunt, mother, and a couple of female cousins fit the bill perfectly. They were dedicated, fast, and honest.

Even the younger kids got into the act. While most were too young for the carnival itself to hire them, several went to work in the "joints." A couple, Chuck and Carol, ran many of the games on the show. We had gotten to know them when my parents let them park their trucks on our property between events. Two of my brothers became "agents" for them making change for customers, calling them in, and restocking when prizes were won.

My youngest brother, seven-year-old Scott, five-year-old

sister Traci, and eight-year-old cousin Rick served as runners, or "go-fers," bringing food and sodas to workers who couldn't leave their posts. Their favorite customers were the flat store operators, who usually let them keep the change from a dollar, even for a thirty-five-cent soda. They also served as "shills" for the game operators, carrying plush animals around the lot as if they had won them. Picture this: a little kid walking around carrying a stuffed teddy bear bigger than he was. If a kid that little could win one, then any macho guy could win one for his girlfriend. And, when nobody else had anything for them to do, they would stand by one of the gut-churning thrill rides to catch pocket change that fell out as the rides flipped the riders upside down. Traditionally, this benefit belonged to the ride operator, but these little guys got to the money that fell outside the ride's fence while the ride boy was still unloading the passengers.

That first year the fair season got underway in mid-July and was concentrated on county fairs in northern California's Sacramento Valley. The largest was the Shasta County Fair in Anderson, California: a typical farming community where American flags flew from every other home, the odor of fresh cow manure constantly wafted through, and schools and churches outnumbered the bars. In Anderson, my ticket box sat just outside the *Himalaya* ride, a monstrous affair that took two trucks to haul. The riders were spirited around a circular track, going backwards past painted scenery purported to mimic Mount Everest and populated by "abominable snow-men," or yetis coated in long white fur. It required two ride operators, one to buckle the patrons in and another who func-tioned as a disc jockey in a booth at the top of the ride plat-form. Screaming into a microphone over the blaring rock music he would ask of the screeching, mostly teenaged riders, "Do you want to go fast? Do you want to go faster? Do you want to go really, really fast?" as he adjusted the ride's speed to their delight.

The *Himalaya* and two other "spectaculars," as they were known, were "independent" rides, owned by someone other than the carnival owners. These mega rides, costing several times as much as most of the others—even the Davises newly acquired *Skydiver*—"hopscotched" from carnival to carnival, operating at only the best fairs, the ones that were sure to fill them throughout the run. The owners "booked" them on for a percentage of the revenue and in turn, the carnival got to pitch them to the fair boards when they were bidding against a competitor.

In the evenings, after it cooled down, crowds flooded the fairgrounds as the locals let loose at the biggest deal the town had going for it all year. Wispy escaping clouds of newly made cotton candy floated through the air. People gorged themselves on corn dogs and other vomit food as they waited to board their favorite thrill ride. The lines at my ticket window were long and unending for three or four hours each night. I almost didn't have time to use my "walks" encouraging techniques, but it didn't matter as the stack of forgotten change grew almost faster than I could push it off to the side to keep space clear for transactions.

By this point my mother had become a virtual hiring hall for carnival workers, as the fairs demanded more workers than the smaller spring still spots. Family members, friends, and friends of friends joined up. Even several of my seminary classmates signed up to help operate rides.

One of them, Charles, drove an old green Plymouth station wagon that our family owned, to haul a few of us. Our memories differ at this point. He says that we left him in Anderson and took the car back with us. I'd always thought he took a bus home, and that's how I got stuck driving that clunker. Either way it happened, I was stuck driving a jalopy full of my younger siblings and cousins on the hundred-and-fifty-mile trip back down through the Sacramento Valley. The problem was that I didn't have a valid, or any other kind, of driver's license yet. I could drive, sort of, but really needed a lot more experience before hauling live human bodies—even small ones, *particularly* small ones—down the middle of America's most populous state. But I was the only available driver, so off we went, one eye on the road and the other looking out for cops in the rear-view mirror.

When we left the Anderson fairgrounds, I was "sandwiched" between the car my mother was driving and my aunt's. The drive went reasonably well on the freeway the first hundred miles or so, but when we got to Yuba City and Marysville, there were things like traffic, stoplights, and left turns.

I got separated from the other two cars. Then, my cousin Vickie decided to start a fight in the back seat. My grip on the wheel got tighter as I tried to drive where I had no business and break up a fight at the same time. I think this is when my hair began to go white. Somehow, I got through the business district before I pulled off to the side of the road. By the time my aunt's car caught up with me, I was about ready to commit "cousin-cide."

After I kicked Vickie out of my car and took about a hundred deep breaths, I was ready to try it again. Aunt Bonnie took Vickie with her, and I was down to two younger kids who were already half asleep. Now all I had to do was learn to drive in the dark.

The last fair we worked that year was in the tiny community of Susanville in California's northeast. It is eighty miles from Reno, Nevada, two hundred from Sacramento, California, and a million miles from everywhere else. Depending on one's perspective, Susanville is either the perfect American hometown or Dullsville, USA. Its Main Street stretches about a mile east to west along California Highway 36 on the way to Lassen Volcanic National Park. The Lassen County Fairgrounds sit on a shaded grassy site at the east end of town, featuring a small grandstand and food booths staffed by the Dairy Wives' Club, the DeMolay, and other civic groups: the perfect setting for a quintessential county fair experience. Even the food was good. My taste buds still remember the Indian tacos.

Susanville was the fair where my cousin Bonnie did her third hand trick.

"How many tickets do you need, ma'am?" Bonnie would ask the customer as she walked up to her ticket booth.

"Ten, please. Six for the big rides and four for the kiddie rides."

"That'll be three dollars and ten cents," Bonnie said as the customer handed her a five-dollar bill. One of Bonnie's hands would take the customer's money while two other hands, held up so the customer could see them, would pull the tickets off the roll and hand them to the customer.

Some people didn't even notice that the ticket girl had three hands. Others just seemed to take it in stride. It was a carnival, after all. But most gawked, nearly forgetting why they were there. And about half of those forgot to take their change. That week Bonnie easily won the "walks" contest.

Bonnie's confederate was scrunched up under the counter inside the ticket box with just one of her hands showing. It seemed to be growing out of Bonnie's belly. Her helper was her little sister Vickie, the same one who had nearly gotten me killed a few weeks before.

The big deal at the Lassen County Fair in Susanville that year was that the carnival owner, Larry Davis, was giving a-way a live pony on Sunday evening just before the fair closed. It was advertised in the fair program and with a big sign near the pony ride. All week long, kids would fill out a form with their names and addresses and put them in a locked box near where the pony was displayed.

On Sunday night the P.A. system announced the drawing. As people gathered, Larry put all the entries into a big plexi-glass tumbler and spun it around. When he drew the first ticket, he announced, "And the winner is... Ricky Elwood," before he realized that Rick was his cotton candy maker's young son. "Sorry, folks. That one has no address, so I'll have to try again." He drew three more tickets from the box before he found one from a local resident. The younger kids in our family, and maybe even Larry's own kids, had spent the week stuffing the box trying to win themselves a pony.

The day after Labor Day, I returned to the seminary for my third year of priestly studies.

But I returned a different person.

I don't know if it was the carnival food or the hard work, but that was the summer that I shot up to my full adult height, finally grasping the brass ring of puberty. But there was more. Throughout grade school and my first two years of seminary, I had bought everything about the religion I was born into hook, line, and sinker. But now I had some life experience of a whole different sort. The carnival was a microcosm. I met people with different lifestyles, different values, and much different ways of looking at the world. But what I met most was compromise, or the reality which required compromise. I didn't articulate it like this yet, though; it was all too new. Back then, I was just beginning to absorb the impact of these new experiences, though my religious armor was clearly getting too small.

I recalled the Good Samaritan story from the Bible. The Samaritan, as far as the Jewish leadership was concerned, was the loser, the carnie of his day; but in the end, he was the guy who did the right thing, the good thing. The Catholic Church was like that. It taught you to be good, what to do to get to heaven. But it was rigid, threatening you with hell if you missed Mass on Sunday.

Theoretically I could crawl out of my tent at daybreak on Sunday morning after working until after midnight the evening before. And I could find a Catholic Church with an early Mass and go back to work on the carnival without fear of going to hell if a ride fell on my head. But it happened less and less frequently; both the getting up early to find a church and the fear of going to hell. And, no ride ever fell on my head.

The carnival certainly never claimed to be as good as the church, but it was more tolerant, more forgiving, more like maybe Jesus was.

When I returned to the seminary in the fall, I kept praying and went to Mass every day. But somehow things were different. I was different. I was still willing to believe what they were teaching me, but more sideways, not quite so absolutely.

But by now I had become accustomed to the seminary and its routine, which could almost not be called a routine because of the way the institution kept changing. But however I could describe it, we kept adapting to it, or else we quit and returned to the life of a regular teenager. My junior and senior years in high school at St. Pius seemed to fly by with little to recall. The action was during the summers at the carnival, which is mostly what I remember from the next two years of my life.

THE BUSINESS BUG

When I returned to Carnival Time Shows the next summer, I had been bitten by the bug. Not the bug of life on the road, but the entrepreneurial bug. I wanted to be my own boss. Some of that circus owner blood, flowing through my veins all my life, was starting to take on a life of its own. It didn't subdue my desire to be a priest, didn't push God out; it just seemed to circulate around the religious part of me in a kind of symbiosis.

I looked around: the carnival boasted glass pitches, balloon darts, basketball tosses, a cat rack, shooting galleries, and the flat stores. The gap in Carnival Time's midway, though, was a ping-pong toss with the prize being, not another stuffed animal, but a living one—a goldfish. The requirements were simple, so I thought: a booth, bowls, ping pong balls, water, and tiny koi. By the time the Anderson Fair rolled around again, I had convinced Larry Davis, the carnival owner, to rent me a booth and let me have the goldfish concession on the show. His only requirement was that I had to have someone else operate the game so I could keep my job as one of his ticket sellers.

After that, I bought some fishbowls and ping pong balls and practiced at home, arranging the water-filled bowls in such a way that enough customers could win a fish, but not so many that it would break the bank. Then, all I needed was just one more ingredient, the koi: the stars of my show.

Talk about your bad timing. The week I had picked to debut my fish business was the same week that goldfish staged a worldwide strike. Let me explain. I started with our local pet store, housed in the Woolworth's downtown on Texas Street.

"I'd like to get two hundred goldfish," I told the salesclerk.

"Just a minute. Let me call my manager."

"Listen, buddy," he said, "I don't know who you are, but we sell our fish for family pets, not some goldfish swallowing contest or whatever you got going."

After I explained to him why I wanted the koi, he was more understanding, not that it helped. "I'm sorry," he told me. "We don't have anywhere near that many fish. I could order them for you, but you can save money by just going over to San Francisco and get them from the same wholesalers we use." He referred me to a couple of places in the City.

So, I trekked over to San Francisco in search of the elusive koi. Turns out, goldfish are foreigners. They come from the other side of the planet; and, due to their delicate constitutions, their preferred method of travel, when not swimming in their own pond, is by air. I don't know if the strike was staged by the airlines, the fish farmers' union, or the goldfish themselves, but there were no goldfish coming in from Asia until the matter was settled. And it would take several weeks at least just to rebuild stocks for their pet store customers if everything went well. So, no goldfish for me.

A less intrepid soul might have given up at this point, but not me; the bug was biting too hard. Bait minnows are about the same size as carnival goldfish and quite abundant in the communities bisected by the Sacramento River, winding its way from Lake Shasta to the San Francisco Bay. In theory, it didn't seem like that much of a stretch. As part of the "flash" (the display) for a goldfish toss, we put various food coloring into the bowls to make them catch the customer's eye and from eight feet away; after all, a fish is a fish. My signs just said it was a fish toss.

I didn't quite get open for Wednesday evening, but by noon Thursday, everything was a go. The booth was erected; a decent supply of minnows was swimming around in the ten-gallon trash can that was their new home when they weren't at work in one of the fishbowls; a couple of my siblings were smartly outfitted with their new change aprons; and the four-inch glass bowls with an opening just larger than a ping pong ball were filled with brightly colored water and carefully arranged, as per my plan.

What could possibly go wrong? Well, how about the sun coming up? And staying up, warming the air, the ground, and the water in my fishbowls. By mid-afternoon on the first day, it was clear that the minnows were risk-averse to spending any serious time in the increasingly hot fishbowls. We first tried rotating them in shifts from the trash can to the bowls, but many of them started swimming upside down anyway, so I was forced to keep the fish that were still alive in the trash can, cooling the water periodically with snow cone ice from the candy wagon.

Plan B hadn't extended to how the customers who won a fish would respond. The lucky winners would get, rather than a goldfish, a minnow in questionable health. Some customers refused their prize outright and demanded a refund. Others carried theirs around but returned if it died before heading for home. Having to replace the fish cut into my profit projections.

Minding my fish joint took considerably more time than I had anticipated, and I took lengthy breaks from my ticket-selling job. By Saturday afternoon Larry let me know that things just weren't working out. He didn't threaten to fire me exactly, as I was the linchpin to a sizeable portion of his workforce, but I got the message. My fish business lasted less than a week. After the fair closed, I returned the booth to Larry and liberated the remaining minnows into the nearby Sacramento River.

But I didn't give up trying to be my own boss.

About a month later we were back in Susanville again. Bud and Sue were the kindly older couple who ran the "garbage joint" on the carnival. They didn't pick up the trash; this is what carnies called the show's souvenir stand that sells balloons, kewpie dolls, and other trinkets. It's the only "joint" where you get what you pay for: a straight-up sale at something approaching a reasonable price. One of the items Bud and Sue sold was giant polka dot balloons fastened to a three-foot flexible reed stick. Twenty-five inches around, they came in a variety of bright bold colors, their complexions studded with yellow and white dots like oversized freckles.

I don't know how I got the idea, but I decided to try selling balloons to the people watching the fair parade that marched its way a mile down Susanville's main street from the post office to the fairgrounds. I negotiated the purchase of a gross [144] of balloons from Sue on consignment; I could return what I didn't sell. I got up early on Saturday morning and found a gas station that let me fill the balloons from the hose it used to inflate tires, and I was on my way. I took a couple of younger siblings to help and was soon walking the mean streets of Susanville, California, looking like a large moving flowerpot, holding a bouquet of giant inflated flowers yelling, "Balloons here. Giant polka dot balloons. Everybody needs a balloon," at people lined up to watch the fair parade.

This new business opportunity held several advantages over my previous effort. It took place before the carnival opened and so didn't interfere with my ticket selling job. It required nothing that had to be kept alive, unless you counted my little brothers. The equipment and investment were minimal, and it was short and sweet. All I needed to do was to get back to the carnival in time to open my ticket box for the "blow-off" from the parade, the influx of crowds that followed the parade into the fairgrounds.

I sold them all, except for a few that broke during inflation and a couple I gave to the gas station guy for his kids as rent for his air compressor.

On Sunday night when the carnival closed, I got paid for my ticket-selling job like always. My pay for working all week selling tickets came to fifty-two dollars, almost to the penny the same amount I had made in my two hours of selling balloons on Saturday morning. It didn't take long to do the math.

***

The next June I thought I was ready to go—be my own boss, direct my own destiny—at least while God was still training me and didn't need much of my attention during the summer. But it wasn't quite as easy as it had been in Susanville.

Running down to the parade for a couple of hours before going to work was one thing but turning this simple outing into a real business was much more complicated. It required capital, supplies, equipment, and employees—even if they were part-time and usually relatives or schoolmates. But mostly it required information. Where were the better parades and when?

And then there was the matter of permission. Who knew small towns could get so uptight about a few teenagers selling balloons for a couple of hours on their pristine byways?

"You need to move along. You can't sell that stuff here," the police officer would say.

"Why not?"

"Because there's a law against it."

"What law?"

"I'm the law."

A single conversation probably never happened exactly like that, but during my parade vending career, I must have heard variations a dozen times or more.

Sometimes the town just wanted a permit, a few more bucks in the city treasury. I quickly learned to make inquiries as to what was required to operate, at least semi-legally. If the license fees were reasonable and the process not too complex, I would comply. But if the answer were simply, "We don't allow that here," I would rebel. I was pretty sure the law was unfair, wrong, and that if General Electric wanted to sell balloons at that town's parade, their lawyers would have made short work of the municipal code. But I wasn't in their league.

I also discovered that even though the city clerk's office might say no, enforcement was spotty. Usually, by the time anybody who was anybody decided that you weren't allowed to sell things at their parade, it was over. It was my version of it being better to ask forgiveness after than permission before. But it was frustrating and sometimes expensive because occasionally we'd be shut down after we'd made the cotton candy, inflated the balloons, and driven fifty or a hundred miles.

The long-lasting effect of this had little to do with parades or making money.

I was born a favored race, a favored gender, was smart, and was able to add to my advantages with a good education. But being told "no" by the police when I knew, or at least suspected, that it was entirely arbitrary, or at the whim of some civic official who had no authority to make such a decision, gave me a sensitivity to people who weren't born with my advantages. Even today, when I hear news of arbitrary police action, or worse, usually towards a minority male, I take considerable offense. Not like some kind of a do-gooder-liberal-white guy who feels sorry for the less fortunate, but in my bones: somebody who has felt it firsthand.

***

In July, Travis Air Force Base staged an Independence Day celebration in an unused field about two blocks away from the monstrous warehouse where my dad worked. Dad was the part of the family who didn't come from the circus. He'd spent his whole working life after the War in the Civil Service on the air base. His rock-solid job matched his rock-solid personality and was about as far from life on the road as you can get. But that entrepreneurial bug even started to infect him.

Dad got me a space at the Travis celebration selling snow cones and cotton candy, my first foray into the food business. Again, I borrowed a booth and a cotton candy machine from Larry on the carnival and hired my cousin Bonnie to make cotton candy. As bands played and fighter planes performed maneuvers in the sky above, and later as that same sky exploded in fireworks, we sold cotton candy and snow cones as fast as we could make them.

When we counted the money the next morning, it came to over nine hundred dollars. After the expenses of product, labor, and paying the Base a commission, I realized that I had made myself five hundred dollars in one day. Five hundred dollars on my first day as a food vendor! That's how much I needed to make all summer to cover my tuition. But I blew it all in one place. That entrepreneurial bug was biting much too strong. Two days later I went to San Francisco and paid cash for my first cotton candy machine; one of several I would eventually own. I would still work at a lot of parades, but the balloons would not be the only item I would sell.

Over the next several years my little business grew. I acquired more cotton candy machines, a couple of trucks, and even a smaller version of the carnival's candy wagon. I hired relatives, friends, and other seminarians. We operated concessions at parades, festivals, rodeos, and rock concerts. One year, Dad helped me buy some used kiddie rides as I tried to get into the carnival business itself—which worked out about as well as the goldfish business.

My two "professions," being a carnie and studying to become a priest hardly seemed to clash. In fact, they usually worked together. I used my seminary credentials to meet and talk to the "committees" that organized the events and persuade them to make me their official vendor. And more than once I remember using the seminary's kitchen to make gallons of snow cone syrup for the next day's parade.

At one event, the Colmo Del Rodeo in Salinas, California, because I was a seminarian, the committee even let me use an old house in town to prepare for their big Saturday night parade. That old house turned out to be the birthplace of Nobel Laureate John Steinbeck of *Grapes of Wrath* fame. I slept in the bedroom where he was born and turned John Steinbeck's childhood home into a temporary cotton candy factory, two years after the great writer's death and just a couple before his birthplace became the well-preserved historic landmark it is today.

On the carnival front, Carnival Time Shows—that little carnival owned by the young couple who had started it less than ten years before—scored big. They were awarded the contract for the "granddaddy" of them all, the California State Fair in Sacramento. The carnival's *Scrambler* ride wasn't the only thing scrambling that year. The Davises probably spent all the money they had and then a lot more to grow their show to state fair size. They bought more rides, recruited more games and food concessionaires, and booked in a dozen of the spectacular rides from the independents. Our family went all out. We all worked at the fair, and Mother recruited some twenty or so new employees for the two-week run.

The Davises first state fair run coincided with the last time it was held at the old State Fairground in South Sacramento. The following year it moved to the new California Exposition Center (Cal-Expo) on the north side of town. Carnival Time Shows held the State Fair contract at the new facility nearly every year until the Davises retired in 1998.

And in a certain way, Larry Davis's presence at the California State Fair has never ended.

***

Is there an adult American who doesn't remember exactly where she was and what she was doing on the morning of September 11, 2001? The events of that day are branded into our souls, as if we had a video camera running inside our heads; one that replays not only sights and sounds, but smells, tastes, and emotions. We see the planes crashing; smell the smoke as it gushes from the wounded towers like a geyser; hear the screams of the trapped victims; watch some jump from one certain death to another nearly a thousand feet below. Even from the West Coast, it seemed, we could smell the acrid smoke invading our lungs, choking us on its death. And we felt shock, horror, sadness, grief—but also a unity, perhaps the last time our country has felt with one heart.

Almost before the smoke had cleared, a man from the West Coast was in New York examining the aftermath, the wreckage, feeling what we all did. He was looking for scraps, some lasting remembrance of our national tragedy that would outlast our individual memories and would speak to those yet to be born on that fateful day. He picked the largest he could find: a one hundred-and twenty-five-thousand-pound twisted steel girder that, like some of the human victims, had fallen tens of stories from the north tower. He had that twisted hunk of metal hauled completely across the United States to the California Exposition [state fair] site in Sacramento, California. Its final few miles it was accompanied by a phalanx of police vehicles and fire trucks, lights flashing and sirens sounding, in honor of the victims the steel memorialized.

That man was Larry Davis, the recently retired owner of Carnival Time Shows, my first boss, and a carnie.

Larry didn't stop with that remnant of the tower's skeleton. Over the next year he had plans drawn, donated his own money, and got other individuals and organizations to do the same; not only people in the amusement industry but contractors, manufacturers, and artisans to complete his "Project of Passion" as he called it. Others refer to it as "Larry's Legacy." Originally opened to the public on Memorial Day 2003, the project was finished by Larry's wife JoAnne after his death in 2006.

As you walk through the main gate of Cal-Expo during the State Fair, your eye catches an anomaly among the food trailers and carnival rides. Just across from the bumper car ride that used to grace Michael Jackson's Neverland, you'll see that tortured hunk of metal surrounded by a quarter-acre plaza of tranquility and history. Beyond that steel, its frozen contortion recalling the faces of the tragedy's victims, both those who died and those of us left, you see a replica of the twin towers, their shimmering blue-tinted skins reflecting the glitter of the carnival neon behind you.

As you climb the ramp that makes the exhibit accessible to all, an unseen curtain descends, blocking out the lights and the sounds and smells of California's annual celebration of itself. You don't smell the deep-fried everything that the squadrons of food vendors offer mere yards away or hear the gleeful screams of the children slamming into one another on the King of Pop bumper cars.

You are drawn to a granite sphere that occupies the center of the memorial. They say it weighs in excess of two and a half tons, but a gentle push with your smallest finger sets it silently spinning on its base, courtesy of the thinnest layer of water molecules. Two elements, stone and water, cooperate to reveal the names of every victim, engraved on that slowly turning ball.

As your fingers gently caress that globe, one sound does intrude. Carillon bells from another tower opposite the Twins chime the hour as you recall, once again, where you were at that other, fateful hour.

The place mesmerizes you, holds you, forces you to revere its every inch. You stand silently in front of the twisted steel beam. You see it, but you also absorb it with all your senses. Its starkness transports you three thousand miles and two decades.

You turn away from the beam as another form beckons you. Its familiar, five-sided, profile again records those who perished there that day: The Pentagon. And finally, a broken wing, gleaming silver, rising as a phoenix from a fountain inscribed with the names of those who gave their lives in a Pennsylvania field so that others might live.

Somehow, it's appropriate, American. A somber tribute to one of our greatest tragedies, set amidst a State Fair. As we celebrate what makes our country great; the bounty of the earth, our entrepreneurial spirit, and our democratic values, the memorial reminds: "Never forget."

A plethora of 9/11 memorials stretch across our country from Ground Zero in Manhattan. But this one, completing the journey from sea to shining sea, is one of the best. A tribute to America and all that She stands for. The inspiration, the money, the passion, did not come from a politician, or religious leader, or a civic group of concerned citizens.

It came from a carnie.

***

Decades after I had first been bitten by that business bug, I was operating the beverage concessions at a Cinco de Mayo event. On Sunday morning I got into a minor disagreement with one of the officials regarding what time we were to open that day. We both insisted we were correct, and the official became frustrated. Pointing to the opposite end of the fairground, to where the carnival was set up, he told me, "You're no better than those people."

No better than a carnie? I could do worse.

PART IV

SMILE, JESUS LOVES YOU

NINETEEN & SIXTY-EIGHT

So much happened the year I started college that that year should have had its own decade. At the very least, 1968 should have come with a warning label: *Caution, open with care. Signed, Pandora*. If the year had been a carnival ride, it would have been the *Zipper*: that gut-wrencher that debuted on Carnival Time Shows that year. It tossed people up, down, and sideways at the same time, spilling loose change, vomit, and the occasional patron to the ground fifty-five feet below—the most dangerous amusement ride ever built.

Before the year had ripped off its first page, the press was reporting that thousands of yellow men in sandals and black pajamas were crawling out of tunnels half a world away from President Johnson's ten-star generals, who gave them no respect. Until they did. Until the Viet Cong's Tet Offensive ripped a ragged hole in America's psyche. Our TV war got serious. We were starting to run short of body bags. We could lose this thing. Losing a war was something that America simply didn't do. The response was more carpet bombing, which was such an easy term, as if we were remodeling somebody's country for them: carpet bomb it.

On the home front, the cannon fodder (a.k.a. America's young people) found it hard to get excited about taking a grand tour of Vietnam to meet the people who lived there. And kill them. They marched, first on campuses and then cities throughout the country. A constitutional amendment short of the right to vote themselves, they persuaded enough of their elders to side with Eugene McCarthy, slushing through the melting New Hampshire snow, to send a message. Like Timothy Leary's buddies, Lyndon Johnson "tuned in," then "dropped out," although there is no record of his ever "turning on."

Spring blossomed like the flowers in the hippie's hair in San Francisco, but love was no longer in the air. Just as it seemed like we might finally overcome centuries of America's Original Sin, a shot rang out in Memphis. The Man with the Dream was silenced by a single bullet. Despite Bobby Kennedy's eloquent plea for calm, thousands of black Americans in tens of cities took to the streets.

Two months later it was Bobby's turn. A few weeks before, I went with some other seminarians to hear him speak in Sacramento. I still have the snapshot I took when I was only five feet away from him. Now that the rules had changed to allow transistor radios, I was listening to the results of the California primary on the night of June 4th.

"And now, on to Chicago, and let's win there," Bobby's words came through the radio around midnight. I continued listening as Bobby started to leave the hotel in Los Angeles. Another man stood five feet from him. His hands held not a camera but a gun. The next sounds I heard were a series of pings and then the cry that Senator Kennedy had been shot. When I heard that it was a .22 caliber gun and that Bobby had asked if everyone was okay, I assured myself that he would be okay as well. But those were his last words, and twenty-five hours later history repeated itself.

In August, at the Democratic Convention in Chicago,

Mayor Daley reminded us why police carry Billy clubs. His police force beat hundreds of young protesters bloody in the streets of that city just blocks from where the politicians were making a mockery of democracy.

But the year ended on a high note, at least for one man. Richard Nixon got back at them for kicking him around. His election, headlined by his secret plan to end the Vietnam War, assured another half-decade of that war, except for the thousands more who died in 'Nam before that last helicopter lifted off the roof of the American embassy in Saigon.

In its own way, the Catholic seminary system was changing as much as the rest of the world. When I'd entered St. Pius X a mere five years earlier, I'd joined a monastic system that had prevailed for hundreds of years. The seminary system was part of the minimal reforms the Catholic Church had instituteed at the Council of Trent in response to Martin Luther's complaints in the mid-sixteenth century. A rigid schedule, and walls—real and figurative—separated future priests from society.

The seminary training program had been divided into two parts: six years for the "minor" seminary beginning with what corresponded to the first year of high school, and the "major" seminary comprising the last two years of college and postgraduate study in theology and pastoral training. St. Pius was a minor seminary serving northwestern California and Sacramento River Valley. We had a high school graduation but returned to the same facility the following fall for two more years.

Except that in 1968 they kicked me out of St. Pius—me and all my classmates. That year, the centuries-old system, suddenly failing, changed. Only four years on from my record-breaking class, enrollment had plunged by half. The logic of expecting a pre-teen boy to know the will of God was beginning to be questioned. And costs were soaring, especially when calculated on a "per priest" basis. Even getting a priest through the twelve years of seminary was no guarantee. A new phenomenon, ordained men leaving the priesthood, often on the arm of a nun, became almost the norm. (Of the sixty-three guys who entered the seminary with me, only two were ordained and only one would make it through a life of ministry to retirement.) Congregants started looking at their priest as less godlike and more human, and the priests started looking at themselves that way as well. Did God really expect them to sacrifice themselves, their manhood, and their sexuality at the altar of celibacy?

The seminary program now consisted of three parts—high school (which ceased to exist five years later), college, and theology—each in separate institutions. Our whole class, its numbers reduced to the low twenties from the sixty-three plus seven who had started five years previous, were transferred to St. Patrick's College in Mt. View on the San Francisco Peninsula.

Back on that former farm in Galt, I'd been pretty much insulated from just about everything, including national and world events and all but the most notable changes coming down from the council in Rome. When a few guys got to keep cars on campus the last year we were there, including my friend Dennis, it was about the biggest deal since John had baptized Jesus in the Jordan River.

But St. Patrick's was different. I met guys from the larger cities of the Bay Area, more sophisticated and worldly than us by far. The buildings were much older than those at St. Pius. They looked like they could house a future-priest concentration camp. But those ivy-covered brick walls with their five-story bell tower belied the life within. We had private rooms and could come and go as we pleased so long as we attended class. A lot of guys even stopped going to daily Mass. Some of our instructors were laypeople, laywomen even. And girls could attend the Wednesday evening community Mass. The room doors all had windows to keep us from inviting girls in or engaging in other unapproved activities, but it was no big deal to hang up an anti-war poster to provide privacy.

Our concern was no longer kitchen raids or sneaking in *Playboy* magazines. Pot was the drug of choice, and even some of the faculty partook. Except for the fact that only males attended, it was like most other small liberal arts colleges. Parties were frequent but usually held off-campus.

But this new freedom belied a new seriousness. Our draft cards were designated 4-D, which told the selective service to skip us, as we'd already been drafted by God. But hundreds of American boys and thousands of Asians were being killed on a weekly basis, and it reached down to us. Priests like Dan and Phil Berrigan were spilling their blood in the same protests where young Americans were burning their draft cards. Other priests—and nuns—were saying with their lives and work that when the words, "Go, the Mass is ended," were proclaimed, it meant we were to go out into the world and do good for our fellow humans.

"Now I say to you that you are Peter (which means 'rock'), and upon this rock I will build my church, and all the powers of hell will not conquer it," (Matthew 16:8). From the first catechism response I'd learned, *"Who made you? God made me,"* religion class consisted of learning and remembering what the Church taught. Everything was really an increasingly sophisticated recapitulation of the authorized St. Joseph's edition of the Baltimore Catechism, approved by the American bishops in 1885, itself merely an update of Robert Bellarmine's catechism of the early seventeenth century.

And it wasn't just me. The Roman Catholic Church considered itself immovable and unchangeable. It was truly a rock, God's rock. And it had been so since Jesus's apostles saw tongues of fire descending on the first Pentecost, nearly two thousand "Years of the Lord" before. But by the 1960s, "rock" meant music, and the rock of the church appeared more like tectonic plates slipping past one another in a sudden cataclysm, unleashing a theological earthquake to rival the geological one in San Francisco in 1906.

We stopped memorizing and started questioning. The seminary itself seemed to be doing what I had started doing myself after my first summer on the carnival. In what was now called theology class, we weren't taught what to believe but were challenged to think for ourselves. While not quite ready to "fuck the establishment" like the students across the Bay in Berkley, we did question everything. The combination of the new thinking, both authorized and not, emerging from Vatican II and the world and national events of the 1960s smashed us right in the face at the same time our genetic adolescent rebellion and testosterone surge was fully kicking in.

I loved it. The new freedom that came with the changes in the church was exactly what I needed. I had a friend whose dad was in the military. Their family motto must have been to follow the rules and not ask questions; but I'd been raised by a circus performer whose motto was, "Rules were made to be broken." So, when we started breaking most of the old church rules and discovered that originally that's probably what Jesus had done—welcoming women, forgiving adulteresses, embracing sinners—I couldn't have been happier.

Perhaps he was not the placard-waving revolutionary I imagined, but Jesus was a long way from the resurrected Christ sitting on a heavenly throne. More rigorous, scientifically focused investigation of Christianity's foundational documents (primarily the canonical scriptures) debunked many of the centuries' old myths and revealed a particularly charismatic human being who found himself siding with the poor, disenfranchised, and marginal people against the religious establishment—the precursor to the religious establishment to which I was training to devote my life.

Suddenly I was confronted by the guy who'd started it all, and it looked like he might not favor the team I was trying out for.

So, I wore my peace signs and my "Smile, Jesus Loves You" buttons with equal reverence, replacing the previous crucifix.

Jesus? "Have you found Jesus?" The evangelical Christians use it as a mantra: the only question that matters. You could rip off your neighbors, even kill a Commie—preferably two—for Christ, and bend most of the commandments back on themselves, just as long as you had admitted that you were born a sinner and turned your life over to Jesus. They'd never acknowledge it, but their system was almost as good as our confessional merry-go-round.

Well, of course I'd found Jesus. I was studying for the priesthood and had been Catholic for as long as I could remember. Or had I?

In Catholic grade school, the nuns talked a lot about God, and the church, and especially Mary. Did I mention that they mentioned Mary, God's mother, a lot? As I thought about it, Jesus, the man who walked around Judea a couple thousand years ago didn't really get that much play. Every Catholic church, classroom, and home had Him hanging from the cross. But I think that may have just allowed us to kill Him again. We had learned about Christ, about God the Son, the second person of the Blessed Trinity. But Jesus, a first-century itinerant teacher? Not so much.

THE DAY THE MUSIC DIED

I got up early on the morning of December 6, 1969. Or would have if I had slept at all the night before. I could do that then, in my college years. At 5 a.m., I backed my 1961 Dodge one-ton pickup into the loading dock at the Pleasanton Ice-house. I pushed a buzzer, and a couple minutes later, the ice man, wrapped in a north pole parka emerged from the freezing, block-long warehouse like the abominable snowman. "Wadda ya want?" he asked, his breath so frosty I could almost read the words coming out of his mouth.

"Snow-cone ice."

"How much?"

"As much as I can fit on this truck."

He returned shortly with a pallet jack loaded with 50-lb heavy-duty brown paper bags of pre-crushed ice. I stood in the back of my truck and he started tossing the bags to me. I stacked them in, four across, until I reached the tailgate.

"How many's that?" he asked.

"Thirty-two, but I think I can get a few more on top."

He continued throwing, and I continued stacking until I felt the springs were ready to rebel.

I paid the man and shoved the truck into gear, heading for the top of Altamont Pass, fourteen miles away. I had just come from there an hour before, and fortunately I knew the back roads. The freeway Highway 580 was rapidly becoming a parking lot. Concertgoers were parking their cars in the middle of that freeway and walking the rest of the way to Dick Carter's Altamont Speedway. Concertgoers; hundreds of thousands of kids and young adults streaming in from all parts of California and beyond. It was a free concert organized by the Rolling Stones; the last stop on their tour and a thank-you to all their fans. Everyone expected it to be "Woodstock West," a continuation of the East Coast lovefest of a few months before, but this time right in the backyard of San Francisco, home of the "Summer of Love."

It was originally scheduled for Golden Gate Park in San Francisco itself, mere blocks from that famous corner, Haight and Ashbury, but the Stones got sideways with the city, and it was moved to Sears Point Raceway in Sonoma. Until two days previous, when there was another falling out. At the last minute, too late to lay proper infrastructure for such an undertaking, Carter offered his track.

Me? I wasn't going for the music. Or the drugs. Or trying to save souls. I had called Dick Carter and gotten myself a spot to park my concession trailer for the concert. The day before, I'd gone with Dad to Oakland to fill his van with cases of peanuts and pink popcorn, a '60s carnival substitute for caramel corn. Kids on pot are not food connoisseurs. We then towed my concession trailer with that same Dodge pickup out to the racetrack, where crews were erecting the stage and dressing tents for the performers. We parked the trailer on a knoll a good quarter mile from the stage and spent most of the night trying to protect our territory so customers could get to the trailer in the morning.

At 4:30 a.m., I went into Pleasanton to get ice, a half-hour drive. The return, with that truck overloaded with ice, took a lot longer. About two miles away, now on a dirt road, I slowed to a crawl. The road was paved with people, toting backpacks, bedrolls, guitars, and an assortment of paraphernalia to go with their drugs.

As I rolled down the window to ask folks to make way, two of them asked me, "Hey man, can we have a ride?"

Before I could say, "No, I'm sorry, but I'm already over-loaded," they climbed aboard.

Nobody else asked. They just got on. It seemed like hundreds but was more like thirty bodies that decorated my truck by the time I reached my trailer. They were already starting their own concert playing guitars, singing, and eating hand-fuls of ice from a couple of bags that had split open.

Most of my family and a few friends were there. We un-loaded the ice, shoving as many of the bags as possible under the trailer to keep it from the day's heat and the crowd. We opened the trailer's awnings, filled the syrup bottles, and dis-played some pink popcorn bricks and bags of peanuts. By 7:30 we were up and running, about six hours before the Jefferson Airplane began playing to kick off the concert.

By ten that morning, business was brisk. The sun was up, and the pot was kicking in. For hundreds of feet around, we were the only place to buy anything to eat or drink. I was out at the van, trying to take a quick nap, when I heard the com-motion.

A group of young people had surrounded my trailer. They reached across the counter and grabbed everything they could get their hands on and threw it to the crowd. As they did so they announced, "We are the Young Communists, and we are here to liberate you from your capitalist shackles." I have to wonder what Lenin would have thought about this, a revolu-tion fought over pink popcorn and snow cones? I did learn something about Communism that day. It's a fast-paced movement. Within less than ten minutes, the Young Com-munists had moved on, apparently to liberate the capitalist musicians. Once we were sure they were gone, we restocked our product and went back to business.

On that December day, Altamont was, both literally and figuratively, the end of the Sixties. Some would eulogize that it was rock music's worst day. Others would just say "good riddance."

Business was good. One of the kids who was roving in the crowd got robbed of a few bucks at knifepoint and headed in a different direction with his next box of peanuts. And slippage, product theft, was a little higher than usual, but not because of any meanness. It was just that they were hungry and particularly thirsty, and many hadn't thought ahead to bring money. Pot, yes; cash, no, although we were offered plenty of pot in lieu of cash. I mean, it's difficult to repossess a rapidly melting cherry snow cone when the customer comes up a little short and may be more than a little high.

We had no electricity, so when the sun went down, we closed, even though the Stones hadn't started their set yet. We put everything away, closed the trailer, and were waiting in the trucks for the crowds to start to thin out.

We could hear the music but couldn't see anything that was going on down near the stage. That's where the trouble was. Wikipedia tells us that "mosh pits" started in the 1980s, but Wikipedia wasn't at Altamont. The stage wasn't high enough. The music was highly "testosteronized." The listeners were high and crushed together. The Hell's Angels were drunk. The mixture proved toxic. One man died. They called it murder, but the court eventually ruled it self-defense. A lot of other people got hurt. There was one drowning due to a drug overdose, although that statistic is surprisingly mild considering the drug-per-square-foot ratio for the day. Two other people got run over as the crowd headed home.

Two years later Don McClean hit the charts with "American Pie." It was the longest song ever to top the charts, its six verses and repeated refrain coming in at over eight minutes.

It was an enigmatic anthem of my generation: The Fifties, when everything was quietly going America's way; and the Sixties, a description-defying decade I lived through, but which I swear had to have lasted much longer than ten years.

But end it did, at that dusty racetrack on that December day. McLean needed a long song for a long decade. His anthem started with an airplane crash taking the life of Buddy Holly, that early rock star so clean-cut even some parents would approve. It ended a decade later, a few hundred yards from where I sat selling snow cones and pink popcorn. It ended with another rocker—Mick Jagger—whose very appearance and clothing mocked everything that earlier decade the Fifties had represented. As Jagger screamed into the microphone the words to "Under My Thumb," one of the Stones' more misogynistic efforts, the Hell's Angels were focused on beating a festival goer, Meredith Hunter, to death with knives, pool sticks, and boots.

They said he was high on meth and was brandishing a pistol, and the Angels were high on beer and misguided machismo, so there were no heroes.

The victims were the music.

And the dreams of my generation.

Those dreams had begun with President Kennedy's words echoing down the capitol mall, "Ask not what your country can do for you but what you can do for your country." And our shared dreams with Martin Luther King Jr. ricocheting back down that mall from the Lincoln Memorial two years later. Dreams shattered by bullets in Dallas, Memphis, Los Angeles, and—always—Vietnam. Altamont symbolized the loss of vision that the Sixties had so hopefully promised. Whether we believed in a religion or not, we believed in goodness. And we believed that we could change the world for the better. And we could do it with love. But it was not to be.

AMY

As the Sixties slipped into the Seventies, the new seminary program required, not that we be locked away from the world, but that we engage with it, to start practicing our ministry skills well before ordination. When I was a junior in college, I helped in a parish in Los Gatos, about fifteen miles from St. Patrick's. I was to serve as a mentor to high school students who met in one of the family's homes each week. We'd sit around on the couches and floor of the living room and discuss the topic for the evening. Often, we'd meander into questions more relevant to teenage lives than the selected religious topic. The program attracted more girls than boys. College-age men, budding celibates, mentoring groups of mostly high school girls—who thought that up? Looking back, it was like sending the fox to the hen house. Perhaps it was the seminary's way of testing our vocation. Not that I was complaining.

One particularly pleasant spring evening, someone suggested that we continue our discussion while walking through the neighborhood. The stars were out, and there was the gentlest of breezes in the quiet upper-middle-class area, so we took up the whole street, eight or ten of us walking side by side.

The second time around the block, I felt a warm feeling in my right hand. Another hand was touching it, and then holding it. The touch was tentative at first, and then firmer, not hard, but in a deliberate, communicative way, like the picture that can speak a thousand words. It was one of the senior girls grasping my hand and pulling me closer to her as we walked along, until our hips and shoulders were touching. It was dark, and I don't think anyone else noticed.

Other than the required "ecclesiastical hugs" at the "kiss of peace" in the new Catholic liturgy, I don't recall having touched a female who wasn't related to me since that long-ago tricycle ride with Tommy, nearly twenty years back. It wasn't for lack of wanting, but natural shyness and the unnatural journey towards celibacy that had held me in check.

The warmth of her hand spread up my arm and into my torso, filling my whole body like the feeling of slipping into a bathtub of warm water. But also, exciting, tingly, like someone had thrown a bucket of ice cubes into that bathtub. We must have circled the block three times in the next half hour or so, but if my life depended on remembering what we'd talked a-bout, I'd be a dead man.

By the time we returned to the house, I had devised my plan. "Does anyone need a ride home tonight?" I got three takers, including my hand holder Amy. In those pre-GPS days, I got lost enough so that I took her home last, not quite know-ing if the hand holding was anything more than just a friendly gesture. Maybe her other hand had been holding someone else's as our group walked through the neighborhood. I pulled up in front of a nondescript two-story house with lights still on in most of the windows. It was a plain structure unlike the more elaborate homes over where our discussion group met.

"My parents are pretty strict, so I better get inside," was the first thing I remember her saying to me. But then, "Would you like to come over for dinner sometime? My mom and I cook a better supper than what you probably get in the seminary."

"Sure," I said. "When?"

"How about next Monday, before the youth group meets? Say five o'clock? You can even come over a little early if you want."

"Okay."

"I'll check with my Mom to be sure. Can you call me? Here's the number."

"I'll do that," I promised and was still saying goodbye as she got out of the car. Then I just sat there, somewhere between stunned and halfway to heaven, as I watched her open her door and disappear.

My car must have driven itself back to the seminary that night as my brain was creating space for a whole new category of thought. I won't mention what my body was doing to me. I was in territory so new and uncharted that I might as well have been clomping through craters on the moon. *Did this actual, age-appropriate young woman really like me? What did that mean? And what was I supposed to do now?* The other part of my brain, where God lived, had already closed for the night. It would re-open later to remind me that I was "called," but on that drive, at least, God left me alone with my fantasies.

What followed was the longest week in human history.

I called her two days later from a pay phone down by Loyola Corners, where I was certain nobody from the seminary could overhear our conversation. She told me that dinner was on. Her Catholic parents were happy to contribute to the nourishment of a future priest.

So now, all I could do was wait for the calendar to do its work. Wednesday is already the longest day of the week—just count the letters. Somehow it got even longer that week, and Thursday and Friday gave it some serious competition. I hope we didn't cover any critical material in class because it's gone. I had a full schedule over the weekend, so the clock sped up a bit. But it made up for it on Monday. From the time I got up until classes were finally over, I was like one of those bored assembly workers watching a frozen clock on the factory wall.

I beat the rush hour traffic and got to Los Gatos in record time. I arrived at Amy's house at 4:15 p.m. and twenty-two seconds. Two urchins opened the front door almost before I finished knocking. They turned out to be siblings number five and six. I told them I was there to see Amy.

"Aaaaamy," they yelled in unison, as if they practiced on a regular basis.

When she came to the door and said, "Hi, Sweetie, come in," I knew I hadn't been mistaken about the hand holding. It was the first time I had really seen her in the daylight. She was almost as tall as me, perhaps an inch or two shorter, and had shoulder-length brown hair with just a hint of curl. Her brown eyes twinkled in a near-perpetual smile. I liked.

"Dad's not home yet but come and meet the rest of the family. They're all here somewhere." The first was her mom Beth, chopping vegetables with one hand, opening the fridge with the other, and yelling at the two kids sitting at the dining table to finish their homework instead of fighting with one another.

"Hello, Mrs. Anders. Thank you for having me over for dinner," I said as she stopped her other activities long enough to give me a hug and welcome me.

"Amy tells me you're going to be a priest."

"Yes, ma'am. Just a few more years to go, and you can call me Father," I joked.

"Well, we're glad to have you. Amy's got a few minutes to show you around before she needs to help me finish dinner. Don't get lost."

We went out to the backyard of their acre lot. As soon as we were out of her mother's sight, Amy took my hand again. They had a good size swimming pool just past the deck at the back of the house. It was separately fenced to keep their barn-yard menagerie out, I guess.

"Let me show you our animals," Amy said. "We're all in 4-H and have projects for the fair in August. I'm raising a lamb this year." By "all" she meant herself and any of her seven siblings old enough to walk and talk at the same time.

We went to the back of the acre lot to inspect her lamb. There was also a pig out there, one of her brothers' projects. Its name was Petunia, even though it was a boy. Amy explained that it would be shown at the fair and then be butchered and frozen for the family table. It was the first time I'd met a pet destined for dinner.

I guess I met all her siblings that day. There were a lot of them, and it was hard to keep track. Whenever my mother noticed other parents with a large family, she'd comment that they were either "Catholic or careless." Amy's parents must have been both, as their brood numbered eight, named following the alphabet: Amy, Brenda, Carl, Danny, Emma, Frank, Greta, and Hanna. It proved a good plan, as I can still rattle off the names of the Anders children faster than I can those of my own brothers and sister.

Dinner was delicious, the best spaghetti I'd ever had. I was the guest of honor, which assured me of the first, and a full, portion but I noticed the pairs of little eyes as I dished up, gauging if enough would be left by the end of the line. Mr. Anders arrived just before dinner was served. He was a driver of some kind, either a short-haul trucker or a delivery guy. I don't recall him saying much that night. He pretty much ate dinner and then sat in his chair.

My summer romance with Amy was like a dog chasing its own tail. I'd hungered for a girl to like me forever, but now that it was happening, I wasn't sure what to do.

Irish guilt, amply supplied by the good nuns, Amy's strict parents, and God peeking over my shoulder prevented us from becoming lovers, but only just. With similar backgrounds, we had a lot in common. We talked about everything, shared confidences, and wrote frequent letters when apart. I even made cotton candy for her high school graduation.

One day, Amy asked me, "Do you know the three kinds of kissing?"

Well, duh. No. I didn't.

"There's 'peaches,'" she said, giving me a peck on the cheek. And then there's 'prunes,'" her puckered lips to mine. God still had too tight a grip on me to try the open-mouthed "alfaaaalfa," which I always regretted.

So, we spent that summer lost in love, under the lemon tree, as Peter, Paul, and Mary crooned, but it was a chaste love.

In mid-summer, on her eighteenth birthday, I began to realize that my fantasy of "having my cake and eating it too" was just that. Birthdays between novios require gifts that speak to permanence and future dreams. I was not able to give the gift that said tomorrow. I knew it, and she knew it.

Shortly after Amy's birthday, my Uncle Rusty asked me to fly up to Medford, Oregon, to drive one of his vehicles back from the Jackson County Fair. It was my first airplane ride, a puddle jumper that made a couple of stops between Sacramento and my destination. I thought I'd have to drive one of his trucks pulling a cotton candy trailer, but I wound up with just his personal car. So, I took a long-cut by way of San Jose to surprise Amy, showing her prize lamb at the Santa Clara County Fair.

My plan worked. I surprised her all right, holding hands with one of her fellow 4-H-ers. In her shock, she greeted me with a "Hi, brat."

I immediately gained ten pounds from the rock that lodged itself in my gut, and the knife sticking out of my chest kept turning. I had no claim, and we both knew God kept me from acting on my desires, but it still hurt—a lot.

After mumbling something about wanting to see if her lamb won a prize, I headed back towards my uncle's car through teary eyes. I put the key in the ignition, but the flood came before I could get it started. I simply leaned against the steering wheel in that dirt parking lot and cried for what seemed like an hour.

I wasn't just crying over Amy. Really, I hardly knew her. Most would say it was puppy love. Sure, it hurt, but that hurt could vanish with a new romance. But what tore at me in the car that day was something more. For seven years in Catholic grade school and another seven in the Catholic seminary, I'd been traveling in a straight line as through a tunnel, towards the priesthood.

But now, I could see the end of the tunnel. It stopped at an impassible rock wall, like the end of a box canyon. The wall was the mandatory celibacy required of priests.

I had known forever that Catholic priests couldn't marry. As a young child it didn't matter. And then, it was a matter of giving up sex. But it was always "I" who was giving up something outside of me, like giving up candy for Lent. That day, in that car, in that dusty parking lot I knew, for the first time, although I couldn't articulate it yet, that what I was going to be giving up in becoming a priest was part of myself. I felt it to the bottom of my soul, even though I yet had no words for what I was feeling.

So, it wasn't just Amy. If I wanted, perhaps I could get her back. Or there would be another. But not if I was going to be a priest. I was turning my back on a big part of myself, something I would always miss, a gaping hole I could already feel tearing at me.

I got angry with God. *"Why God, why? Why do you want me to be a priest? Why not get somebody else? There's plenty of guys who don't even like girls. For Christ's sake leave me alone. Let me have my life."*

But maybe it wasn't God. Maybe it was the Catholic Church. That's where the rule came from. The Church said you had to be unmarried to be a priest. *"But why?"* I knew how it had started, way back when. Priests used the parish as their own fiefdom and passed it on to their sons. Holiness or care for the people had little to do with it. Plus, a married priest, with legal or at least squatter's rights to his own parish, was less beholden to the bishop and the bishop's king.

And I knew the official line since Vatican II, just a few years ago. Celibacy was a "gift from the Lord." We were to be unmarried, like Jesus. It would make us better priests, save us from dividing our time and focus between family and ministry. Not having a wife was supposed to make us more available to our flock.

My hands death-gripped the steering wheel of the old Buick. *"Bullshit! Bullshit! Bullshit! It was about power and control. They had us by the short hairs. We weren't that much different than the 'castrati' in the old Vatican Boys Choir."*

I left that dusty parking lot that day a different man. I still felt that God was calling me to be a priest. I still wanted to become one. And I still thought I would make a good one. It was my relationship with the Church that had changed. I gave myself permission to challenge its teachings, not just about priestly celibacy, but other things, nearly every other thing. "Holy Mother Church" was a phrase no longer in my vocabulary. I suppose my more adult, skeptical faith had been growing for several years, but that day was a milestone. From that day, everything the Church taught, or asked of me, had to be filtered through reason and balanced against the values and teachings of its founder, Jesus. My faith wasn't as simplistic as WWJD, "What would Jesus do?" but that is a simple way of explaining it. The crunch I heard backing out of the fair parking lot were the tires flattening more of my faith armor.

The letters between Amy and myself had stopped, and I licked my wounds for a few weeks. After school had restarted, me in my last year of college, and she in her first, Amy and I met a few more times. One afternoon, sitting in a park, overlooking a small lake, she laid it out for me.

"Nove," she said, "I really like you. I think you know that. But my future is to have a husband and a family. It's something I want more than anything. You've seen me with my little brothers and sisters. I've practically raised half of them. It's what makes me feel alive."

I listened with my ears and from someplace else deep inside but said nothing.

"I know God wants you," she continued. "I want you too, but I know I can't take you away from God. It wouldn't work for either of us."

I nodded, knowing she was right as I watched the tears gently flow down her cheeks, matching the ones I felt on my own face.

The last time we met, she told me about a young man, Phil, with whom she worked at her part-time job out at the Frontier Village amusement park. She thought he was a "keeper," and she was right, as they remained married for almost forty years. As she hugged me goodbye that day she said, "Let's keep in touch."

***

We didn't, really.

Over the next thirty-five years I saw Amy exactly twice. We exchanged Christmas cards a couple of times and an occasional note, but that was all. I don't recall if we ever even had a phone conversation.

We reconnected about five years before her death. At that time, my mother's health was failing, and I had begun making trips to California every two or three months to visit her. Having lived in Washington for many years, I had lost contact with the people I had known growing up in Northern California. I took advantage of my travels to find some of them. I didn't know what had become of Amy and Phil as they had moved from the last address I'd had, but I found one of her brothers and got a phone number.

She was glad to hear from me. That same evening, I met

Amy and Phil for dinner at a restaurant in San Jose. Over the next few hours, we exchanged life stories. Much had happened to both of us, but in some way, it seemed like three and a half decades had not intervened. On my next visit I invited her parents to join us, and yet another time we were joined by Patti and Cathy, two of the other women from the high school church group she had been attending when we'd met.

The fourth time that my travels enabled me to visit Amy was the day before Halloween in 2008. Phil was working that evening, and Amy and I had dinner alone at a restaurant in San Jose. As we walked back towards my car, she took my hand once again in hers. That's when she said the C-word to me, as in "Cancer sucks," or on particularly bad days, "F**k cancer." She had just learned that breast cancer, which she had thought she had beaten some five or six years before, had returned; and this time was not curable.

Over the next three years, I visited Amy as often as my schedule would allow, some dozen or so times, each of which I hold as a treasure. On two occasions when I called, Phil informed me that she was feeling too poorly to see anyone. Usually, I came to her home, visited a while, and then took whoever was around to dinner. I got to know all her children and made friends with her grandson Andy. Long forgotten by me, I had promised her a trip to San Francisco when we were young, and I finally fulfilled that pledge. Twice, I visited her in the hospital, and there met her youngest sister and advocate Hanna, whom I had last seen when she was a three-year-old. Phil was cool, although after her death, in thanking me for my kindnesses, he acknowledged that at first, he'd felt uncomfortable by Amy's rekindling of our friendship. I understand that I had always been referred by her to her kids as "the guy before Dad."

I attended two of Amy's fifty-nine birthdays, both bittersweet occasions. On the first, her eighteenth, I began to realize that I could not please her and God both. Forty years later I attended another birthday party, less intimate, taking up half a county park for Amy's three hundred closest friends. I bought a four-foot card, which everyone signed, knowing that as we penned our names, we were all saying goodbye in one way or another.

I only got the word of Amy's death in time to get from Washington to California for two of the four services that celebrated her life. She managed to live until she died, going out to lunch the day before lying down for the last time. During the night, while her husband and sister nodded, the angels came.

The two services I attended had been meticulously planned, by Amy, of course. At St. Julie's, where Amy and Phil had long been involved in the Cursillo community, a Catholic spiritual renewal movement, over five hundred people showed up. Even coming from Washington State, I was not the farthest traveler. The emotionally charged service ended amidst gentle song and luminaria in the church courtyard as the stars twinkled their encouragement.

The official funeral, known in Catholic circles as the Mass of Resurrection, was the following evening at a packed St. Mary's, the parish of Amy's birth and where we had met. The hearse, bearing Amy's ashes and her family, was ushered down the staid streets of Los Gatos by her son-in-law's HOG group, their unmuffled exhausts shattering the village's tranquility. They were met on the church steps by a military color guard arranged by her Air Force Iraq Vet son and the local chapter of the Blue Star Moms. Amy was going out in style.

Tears—apparently my ears were crying too—prevented me from hearing much of the eulogy that Phil offered for his love of forty years. But his opening words said it all. My name is... "Amy's husband."

FIGHTING WITH GOD

In my last year of college, Fr. Ed Miller had been appointed as my spiritual director. We were to meet weekly to discuss progress in my growth towards the priesthood.

"Father, I can no longer accept something the Church teaches," I said at our second appointment.

"That's normal, Nove. We all have our doubts from time to time," he counseled. "It will pass."

"I don't think so, Father. This is a big one, and I've been thinking about it a lot."

"Tell me what it is, and we'll talk about it. I'm sure I can help you."

"I don't agree with the church's teaching that priests can't be married. I mean, why would God care?" I asked.

"Well, God has His reasons, which are beyond our knowing. If God calls a man to be a priest, then he also gives him the charism, the gift, to live life as a celibate."

"But the ministers in other religions can get married and still serve God."

"They're Protestants. They don't have the 'fullness' of the priesthood. It's not the same," he said, his face beginning to redden.

"But what about the Eastern rite priests? They're Catholics. They can marry."

"You want to become an Eastern rite priest? Go back to the old High Mass that takes two hours? Say Mass in Greek? Grow a long beard? Is that what you want to do?" he asked, starting to raise his voice.

"No, of course I don't want to do that, Father. I just want to be a priest and have the chance to get married if I ever choose to do so. And I don't think that God cares one whit. In fact, maybe He really prefers that we marry. Maybe we'd be more understanding, be better priests," I wagered. "I think that celibacy is just the Church's rule, you know, to control us."

At this last comment, Fr. Ed's face turned bright red, and his voice could be heard out in the hallway. "Don't talk like that. Don't even think that way. The pope, the American bishops, they all teach that God gives the gift of celibacy to those He calls to the priesthood. He wants us to be unmarried like Jesus so that we are more available to serve His people like the fathers at Vatican II taught us."

"Then how can you explain that it says in the Bible, the Word of God, that Peter's mother-in-law was ill? If he had a mother-in-law, he must have been married. And it was Jesus himself who called Peter," I retorted, knowing I was on a roll, "to be the very first pope."

Fr. Ed heaved a deep sigh. "I've done my best to tell you Holy Mother Church's position on this subject. It's from God. It won't change. You need to think about that. You need to listen to God. Maybe he's not calling you to be a priest after all. I know that he gives the gift of celibacy to those of us he really calls. Think about it. And, if you still believe in prayer, pray about it. We'll talk more next week."

Fr. Ed's somewhat implied threat didn't worry me. But it got me thinking. My soul knew he was wrong but what did it matter, his opinion or mine? The rules, fair or not, wrong or not, were the rules. And the circus in me didn't like rules. But if I wanted to be a priest, I was going to have to follow the rules.

So, I came up with a plan. In a few months, I'd be graduating from college and after that, I'd be moving over to the Theologate in Menlo Park for my last four years before ordination and the promise never to have sex. Why not take a break, a year off, not for discernment, not to try to find out if I really wanted to be a priest, but just to have fun? I'd go to Europe, for sure, and maybe get a VW "hippie van" and travel across America on the way. And the biggest item on my "fun menu" would be meeting girls. Young women, American and European, in various flavors would do just fine. If I was going to have to give them up for life, what was the harm in having a taste first. In fact, something inside me almost demanded it.

Fr. Ed was also my biology teacher. That quarter, I got a "D" in biology, the only "D" I ever received in my entire academic career going back to first grade.

The following year, Fr. Ed left the priesthood to get married.

***

But I did what Fr. Ed asked. I prayed about it. It went something like this.

"God, we need to have a talk."

I could've gone to the chapel and knelt by the altar or sat in one of the back pews. Or maybe taken a walk down by the grotto. But I wanted to do this on my own turf, so I sat sideways on the partially made bed in my room, with my legs stretched across the spread and my back leaning against the wall.

"I know you've wanted me to be a priest for a long time, about as long as I can remember. And that's been fine with me. I know I didn't have a particularly good idea of what it was all about when I was a kid, mostly appearances and positive feelings. And I must tell you, after Fr. Luke read us the riot act, and practically threatened to rip us a new one on that first day at St. Pius, I had my doubts. Whatever image I had of what a priest was supposed to be, he pretty much shattered that. And the other priests there, with their foibles showing through their cassocks, like holes worn in the fabric, didn't offer much help. So, I don't know why I hung in there for all these years. You, I guess."

I re-adjusted my position on the bed and went on.

"But these last couple of years, in college, it has become a lot clearer. In the end, it's really about love. And a particular kind of love, a giving love, caring about people, listening, healing them, providing encouragement. And it's reaching out into society, taking risks, challenging people, and myself to be better, to treat one another like You want us to. I used to think Mass, the Eucharist, was some magic ritual, but now that I'm older, and especially since the altars got turned around and we look at one another, I understand a lot better. We gather and remember the example of Jesus and encourage each other to be as much like him as we can. And then go out a try to make the world a better place.

"So, sure, I want to be a priest, and to lead communities in making things better. And I think I'd be a damn good one— oops, sorry. Other people think so too. You remember Megan, that tall, skinny, too skinny, girl with the stringy blond, almost albino white hair, from the youth group? Of course, you do. You made her. She was hit and miss, sometimes even coming to song practice but not showing up for the Youth Mass later that same day. Some of the other girls said it was because she was a lesbian, and her parents had kicked her out. She didn't talk much, so I don't really know. But when that girl played that violin of hers, Beethoven's 'Ode to Joy' after communion, it sent chills down everybody's spine, probably even Yours.

"Anyway, she came to the last retreat we had up off Highway 17 on the way to Santa Cruz. I was wearing that old black hat I'd gotten somewhere. It wasn't anything special, but I liked it for some reason. So did Megan. Saturday afternoon we were talking, first time I remember her saying much at all. She told me she liked my hat. Without thinking, I took it off and gave it to her. 'It's yours,' I said. That's when she looked me right in the eye with that strange look of hers and told me, 'Nove, you're going to make a good priest.'"

I stood up and walked around the room, as I was getting to the serious part.

"I mean, that's just one example, God, but there've been others. Another girl, Amy, she knew you wanted me to be a priest. She wanted me too for herself but turned loose of me so I could follow you. But that was hard, God, really hard. I like Amy, a lot. I wanted to go all the way with her. Not in the sexual sense; well that too—you're God, so no use lyin' about it. But mostly like, with a family, kids, a life together, maybe. But we couldn't even find out if it were possible because you want me to become a priest. And, as you know, she's a good Catholic girl, so what could she do? You can't fight City Hall, and you sure as hell—sorry again—can't fight God.

"Which brings me to what I mainly want to talk to you about: celibacy. To be blunt, I don't like it. Until Amy, I guess I never gave it much thought—just part of the deal. Now Fr. Ed, he says that if you want someone to be a priest, you make it so they are okay with celibacy. But I gotta tell you, God, I'm just not buying it. Too many guys are quitting and getting married. And some of the best priests too, like Fr. Jim. Now I'm not blaming you. I don't think you set it up that way. I think it's mostly from Rome. I know there were some problems, like hundreds of years ago, but it's different now. And I just think, to be frank and pardon my French, that forcing priests to be celibate is just a big pile of doggie doo."

What the hell was I doing talking to God like this? Like we were on a first-name basis? I drew in a deep breath. No lightning struck anywhere near me. Either God wasn't listening, or He was, and what I was saying was okay with Him. Maybe He wasn't too keen on the celibacy thing either. It had been a long time since I believed God talked out loud. He gave signs, so I now thought, and you had to look for them. The lack of lightning striking seemed as good a sign as any. So, I kept going.

"Now I'm not asking you to do anything. I'm not one of those people who pray to you to fix every little thing or expect you to move the tornado a block away, so it hits somebody else's house instead of theirs. I guess people would call me a 'deist' like Thomas Jefferson. As far as I can tell, God, You got things going and then have left it up to us to handle it on a day-to-day basis. I'm pretty much hoping that with so many good men quitting, they'll change that stupid rule before too long. And since it's just You and me talking, maybe they'll let women be priests as well.

"In the meantime, here's my plan, and I hope it's okay with You. I'm gonna take a little break after I finish here at college before I go on to Theology over in Menlo Park. And I'm gonna come back and get ordained to be a priest—and a good one, I hope. But God, if I ever meet another woman and have the same feelings I have about Amy, I'm not gonna let her get away. I'll marry her, and if I have to give up the priesthood to do it, that's how it'll be if they haven't changed the rules by then.

"I hope You'll understand. Thanks for listening."

REVBOB

Still smarting from having to give up Amy, I wasn't going to go back to the youth group at St. Mary's. I looked for another service project for my last year of college. I first tried visiting the kids in juvenile hall in San Jose, but that required wearing a clerical collar and looking like a junior priest, which didn't fit with my current anti-clerical approach to life. Even though I was still planning to become a Catholic priest, I was pissed off with the church and many of its trappings.

A note pinned to the bulletin board outside the chapel said that a Rev. Robert Herhold was looking for someone to help him with a new ministry he was starting, an outreach to young adults in the apartment cities that were springing up in what would soon be known as Silicon Valley. I called the number, made an appointment, and showed up at the end storefront in a new strip mall that "RevBob," as I came to think of him, had rented and creatively named *The Christian Community*.

"Hi. I'm Bob," the reasonably tall, kindly-faced man said, skipping all the formalities.

"My name's Nove."

"So, you're studying over at St. Pat's. How long you been

there?"

"This will be my third year, but it's my eighth in the seminary."

"Are you going to be a priest for San Francisco or a religious order?"

"Neither," I said. "I'm studying for Sacramento. I just transferred here when they changed the system. Next year I'm scheduled to go to Menlo Park to start Theology."

"Well, welcome. Let me show you around, although there's not much to see." He was right. The space was rather bare, not church-like at all. Two sides of the corner space exposed to the parking lot were all windows. There were a couple of wire book racks with books for sale and lend. A table against the wall held clipboards with sign-up sheets for various activities. Most of the space was open, surrounded by a circle of folding chairs with more stacked against the wall. In the far corner Bob had set up a little counseling space with a small desk for himself. There may have been a simple piano that I don't remember, but I doubt it. The population that Bob was aiming for preferred guitars. And there had to have been a cross hanging somewhere, but I've forgotten where it was.

We sat down in a couple of the chairs to continue our conversation.

"I've got a year off—two if this works—from my denomination and some funding for my mission. I want to reach out to the unchurched young adults who live and work around here. It's not so much that I want to convert them to anything, but I'd like to get them in touch with the spiritual part of themselves, convince them that life is about more than worldly success. And I want to challenge them. A lot of our activities right now are about protesting the war."

Wait a minute. Did he just say "denomination"? This guy's not a priest? He's not even Catholic. Christian? I'll grant him that, so far.

Ever so casually, I asked, "What denomination do you belong to, Bob?"

"Oh, I'm a Lutheran pastor. But we're losing members like so many other mainline Protestant churches, and we just aren't attracting the young. I don't think it's happening in the Catholic church yet, probably because of Vatican II, but it will. And you know better than I do that the priests and nuns are already leaving in droves."

"You're right about that," I said.

"I'm in my forties, and I feel that I need a couple of younger guys to help me, maybe who can relate better to these younger adults. I've already got another guy, Gordon. He's a seminarian like you; well, not exactly like you. He spent some years in Divinity school, non-denominational, and just got back from two years in the Peace Corps. You'll like him, if you join us.

"I asked one of the young women who comes here and goes to your Wednesday night public Mass if she'd put up a notice for me. I'd like to add a Catholic to the mix. I think that prayer and liturgy are an important part of spirituality and community building, and nobody does liturgy better than the Catholics.

"So that's it. What do you think? We meet here once or twice a week and then outside events as they come up. I'd like someone who could be here for most of our gatherings."

I'd come a long way since I'd believed that going into a Protestant church would send me to hell. But working with a Protestant minister? That was a step further. But that's a big part of what the Vatican Council taught, Ecumenism, reaching out to people of other faiths. And I liked this guy. He seemed more sincere and was talking a lot more like what I thought the Gospel was about than many of the priests I'd met over the years. So, why not?

"I'd like to give it a try," I told RevBob.

Over the next few weeks, I met Gordon and some of Rev-Bob's regulars, and I took flyers to the local apartment complexes to try to get new people to join us. We didn't exactly hold services. It was more like discussion groups—sharing sessions, which were popular at the time.

The first time I remember something that would qualify as a religious service was around Thanksgiving. We had gathered for a potluck dinner, most of the dishes having come not from the kitchens of single young adults but from the deli section of the local grocery co-op. After eating we sat in a circle and shared our stories of thanksgiving—things we were grateful for. The recollections were interspersed with short readings from scripture and other sources which RevBob would have someone read. I think there was some singing, although I may have that confused with the Christmas party in December.

Then, as we sat in that circle of folding chairs, RevBob took a round loaf of San Francisco sourdough and held it in his hands while he recounted Jesus's actions at the Last Supper. "This is my body, given for you. Take and eat." He broke the loaf in rough halves and started to pass it around the circle indicating that we were each to tear off a portion.

I took my share, but I held back. I remember floating outside of myself above the group. I saw me, and RevBob, and Gordon, and the others; people I'd come to know and care about. It was unmistakable. We were celebrating Eucharist, what Catholics call "Mass," but I couldn't quite give myself to the moment.

And why not?

Because of God, the pope, and the Catholic teaching that had been brainwashed into me since before I could remember. The Eucharist, the Mass, was a re-enactment of the Last Supper, and Catholics believed that when we broke and shared the bread, even if it usually looked and tasted like plastic, we were really eating Jesus's body. Literally. When the priest, a Catholic priest, repeated Jesus's words, the bread and wine changed into Jesus's body and blood. It was real, not symbolic like the Protestants believed. The medieval theologians had even invented a new word for it: "Transubstantiation." When the Catholic priest, "alter Christus" (i.e., another Christ), said the words of consecration, the bread and wine stopped being what they had been and became Jesus's body and blood. The "accidents" of bread and wine, the look, feel, and taste remained. But the "essence" or "substance" became something else: the body of Jesus. Hence "Trans-substantiation." It's what Catholics believed, or told themselves they did. This, and following the pope, was what mostly separated us from the Protestants.

And, as much as I'd come to respect him, RevBob was still only a Protestant minister, not a Catholic priest. As Fr. Ed had said, he didn't have the "fullness" of the priesthood. So, this wasn't really the Eucharist, not *really* the body of Jesus.

My heart knew that I shouldn't feel this way. Everything we were doing was true to what I was coming to believe Christianity was all about: loving, sharing, living the values of Jesus. Even my head agreed. The new theology I was learning stressed that it was the participants who were becoming "the body" of Christ when they came together to break bread. It was about what happened to people, not to bread and wine.

But something held me back. The now nearly-grown-up me still couldn't make the break with the Catholic tradition I was raised in. I felt bad. Like doubting Thomas, I wanted to believe in this new meaning of Eucharist—of Christianity, of humanity—but I just couldn't, not quite, not yet. After all, I was almost eight years into studying to be a Catholic priest, the one who *could* turn that bread and wine into Jesus's body and blood.

***

One of the things that somehow hadn't crossed my mind when I agreed to help at Christian Community was that a fair number of the young adults, we would be working with were likely to be women. Well, duh. What had I not been thinking?

And they were a bit older, and more "experienced" than the girls in the youth group.

And, not still living with their parents.

I imagine that some of them could have chewed up and spit out a guy with my lack of experience. Like the two stewardesses who came to our first retreat. Those were the days when stewardesses were in the "coffee, tea, or me" and "we really move our tails for you" mold and had to pass the bar for beauty, age, etc. If one or both of them had decided they wanted to test my vocation, I would probably have followed them anywhere. I might have become a member of the "mile high club" before I'd even lost my virginity. It occurred to me that if my plan now were to have a "fling" after college, before I hunkered down to some serious celibacy, there was no reason to wait until graduation. Other than a woman named Claire, who would go after anything that was male and moved, the women who came to the storefront church didn't exactly wait in line to throw themselves at me. But the "priest thing" intrigued some of them. What made a guy like me tick? Did it pose a challenge, or did they want to protect my virtue from other predatory women?

***

Good Friday found several of us from the Christian Community including Gordon, myself, and RevBob joining other anti-war protesters at the gates of the factory in San Jose, which manufactured cluster bombs. These anti-personnel "bomblets" are notorious for continuing to explode and cause devastation and death decades after the conflicts for which they were deployed ended. Fortunately, in 2010 the world banned their use. Unfortunately, the United States is still not a signatory.

We stood outside the locked gates of the plant, owned by Honeywell Industries. The gate was probably standard chain link topped with concertina wire, but when I picture it in my mind today, I see the *Arbeit Macht Frei* gate at Auschwitz. We stood in silence. We prayed. We read scripture passages. I read a selection from the end of John's gospel about Jesus's trial and crucifixion.

As we were leaving, a young man came up to me and said, "I'm Jewish. That passage you just read from your Christian Gospel disparages my people. Did you know that? I wish you had chosen something else to read."

After I got back to the seminary, I re-read John's account of Jesus's passion and death. The man was right. Throughout his account the Evangelist sounded like he was criticizing the Jews, blaming them for Jesus's death. And then I remembered what my mother had frequently said about her daddy, the circus owner. He'd always referred to the Jews as "Christ killers." I realized that it had been nearly two thousand years of such thinking that had brought the world to those gates at Auschwitz just a few decades previous.

***

Then it was the Christian Community's spring retreat at Half Moon Bay. It was late Sunday morning, and we'd be leaving in a couple of hours. We were sitting down by the beach, but not right on the sand. There are a few more than a dozen of us, but not as many as two dozen. We were recapping some of our discussions from the weekend, always trying to make more sense of life. I think Gordon had been telling some of his experiences from the Peace Corps. Those of us who had gone to the last peace march in the City expressed our anger and frustration at the never-ending war and our sadness at the lives being lost. Nearly everybody knew someone who had been killed or knew someone who knew of someone.

We prayed. We read a bit of scripture. We held hands around a circle as RevBob lead us in the Lord's Prayer. Then he began to pull the loaf apart, and we passed it around, each tearing off a chunk. We ate. I'd long ago stopped worrying over what happens to Jesus when we chew the bread, or what may happen to a seagull who might pick up a crumb—no gold *patens* here. In a few years I expected to find myself holding this same bread and saying, in English now, "This is my body." But I wouldn't be talking to the bread. I'd be addressing my words to the community gathered around me.

I looked over at RevBob and saw a priest. I saw myself in a few years. In these last few months, the distinction between priest and Protestant minister had evaporated. I realized that I couldn't find it if I tried.

I took in a deep, quiet breath. The ocean air filled me to my soul. I remembered my reservations at the Thanksgiving Eucharist just a few months before. I thought of my accordion lessons in that little Protestant church. So long ago, centuries probably.

There was almost nothing left of my old faith armor. I left almost the last chunk of it on that beach. Almost, but not quite the last little bit. That was still to come.

The revelation humbled me. How could I have missed this all these years; been so wrong? What else did I still need to learn? I knew that priests weren't what I'd thought at all. And now, men who weren't priests at all suddenly were. Jesus was a man. God? Maybe, but a man certainly. The big sins were now little sins, if they remained sins at all. The big sins had different names now: war, violence against the weak; corporate greed; racism; and soon, sexism.

The Commandments had taken second place to the Beatitudes. The Church's mission had changed, it seemed to me, from saving souls for heaven to saving the world from itself. And I was glad to be part of that. As I looked across that circle of sand at RevBob and looked around at that small group that dared to call itself the "Christian Community," I wanted to be a priest then more than ever.

LAURA

The third and final retreat I attended with "the Christian Community" was held in Santa Cruz a month after I had graduated from college. We first met at our storefront and carpooled to the beach. While waiting for the others to arrive, I noticed someone new browsing the bookrack. It was a young woman, college-age, her dirty-blonde hair parted into two pigtails in the back—just a touch of hippiness. I chatted briefly with her.

"I'm here with my mother," she told me. Alice was someone I had previously met, a woman my parent's age, and not our usual participant. She had come from an unchurched family and had been widowed when her youngest daughter was only thirteen. That daughter, the young woman at the bookrack, had recently become a Christian during her first year away at college, and her mother wanted to learn a bit more about it so she could be closer to her daughter. It was the mother's idea that they come on the retreat together. How many times, over the years, would I ask myself, *what if* she hadn't?

Saturday afternoon found us all sitting around in the living room in one of the two houses that RevBob had rented for the retreat. We were sitting on couches and chairs, and on the floor, and on those oversized beanbag pillows that were popular at the time.

"What I'd like to do today," RevBob said, "is to go around the room and introduce ourselves but with a twist. Tell us, as best you can, about your 'faith journey' so far. What part, if any, does God play in your life? What questions do you have? I'll start."

RevBob's story was pretty much your typical "boy meets God" tale, like my own, except Protestant, and without the elephants and the carnival rides. The most interesting part, I found, was that he, a Lutheran minister, was married to a woman who was an atheist. That should have made for some interesting bedtime conversation.

We went around in a circle. I don't remember what the next couple of participants said but then it was the new girl, Laura's turn.

"It all started with my Dad's death six years ago. I felt it was my fault. Ever since we'd moved back from L.A. he'd been stressed. Then he lost the new job we'd moved up here for, and that's when things really got bad. Mom hadn't wanted to move, and to make matters worse, Dad had bought our house without even showing it to her first.

"I retreated to my room with my music, but I guess I played it too loud, even in my room. Dad constantly yelled at me to turn the music down. One day, about a week before, he just lost it. He stormed into my bedroom, jerked the plug from the wall, and smashed the stereo to the floor. A few days later he fell over with the stroke. He was in the hospital five days before we had to pull the plug."

Her voice was quiet, low, and nearly flat emotionally. Nobody moved or said anything as she continued.

"I felt guilty. I knew I had killed my dad. I was sad for my mom. It was just me and her. My sister, five years older, had already had enough with Dad. She'd moved out, was off to college with her friends, her life, her new boyfriend. So, it was just us, me and Mom. She was devastated, lost. It was my fault, and I was the only one left to be with her in her grief.

"I felt the guilt, and my mom's sadness, but I don't know that I really grieved my dad's passing. In a way, which added to my guilt, I was glad he was gone. It made life hard, but somehow it made it easier too."

(Although I listened with compassion then, I could not have known that it would be another quarter-century before her soul would release the memories of the sexual abuse.)

"Mom's over in the other house, taking a nap right now, so that's why I can tell you this. I hope you'll understand. As the Reverend says, it's just for us in this room to hear.

"High school was anything but easy. I was the new kid on the block. I had no Dad. And the house he'd picked out was in a neighborhood we really couldn't afford. Plus, I was the only one to be there for Mom.

"The things I did just to take care of me were probably the wrong ones, a few drugs, a little bit of sex. Nothing too bad, but nothing too good either.

"But I'm smart, and I liked school. When it was time for college, I started out at the local community college. I was making a few friends, real ones, but I wanted to go to a college where I could get a degree. It was a huge stretch, but I talked Mom into letting me go away to Oregon."

She began to speak of her "faith journey" as if she hadn't been already.

"Our family was never really religious. Mom had happily left her Southern Baptist roots behind her when she moved out to California. I went to Sunday school here and there, probably for the social part because my friends went.

"At college, I live in a dorm with other women, several of whom have become good friends. One of them is Christian, and I started going with her to the campus ministry prayer group and to the church she attends. The minister said that Jesus loved us, had died for us. Jesus loves me? I wasn't so sure.

"One day I was sitting in the window of my dorm, two floors up. I had a rose in my hand—Portland is the City of Roses, you know. I absent-mindedly pulled the petals off the rose and chanted the child's song under my breath, 'He loves me, He loves me not,' thinking of what the minister said about Jesus.

"As I watched the last petal settle in place on the lawn twenty feet below, I noticed something. The fallen rose petals had arranged themselves into the pattern of a cross: Jesus's answer to my question.

"And that's my faith journey. I've been going to an Episcopal parish since I've been home this summer. I like their liturgy. It makes me feel closer to God. And I feel that I want to do something special with my life. I want to love the world."

I want to love the world.

That was essentially what I wanted to do too. Not that I had that much experience in deep conversations with women my age, but I had never heard a woman speak that way. Somehow, I had tied up all considerations of altruism with the Catholic priesthood. Yet here was someone, not even a Catholic, who was thinking some of the same things. Most importantly, she was a *she*, a female, someone the pope had infallibly declared could never be a priest. *So sayeth God the Father.*

I wanted to know this woman better. That evening I persuaded her to take a beach walk with me.

"Have you always wanted to be a priest?"

"Pretty much."

"That's a bit unusual."

"Suppose so."

"And what about the circus stuff you mentioned? How's that fit in?"

"Well, my family were circus owners for three generations. Guess you could say I was born wearing clown makeup and a silver cross in my mouth."

"What?"

"Oh, just trying to make a joke. Guess it didn't work."

"I don't know. I don't get most jokes. I take things literally. I'm gullible. If you tell me something, I'm probably going to believe you."

"Sorry. Tell you what. I'll get me a T-shirt with a big 'K' on it for 'kidding' and open my shirt, so you'll know. By the way, that's another joke."

"I love this place," I said, "Santa Cruz. The ocean, the waves, I think there really is something primordial about it. I can almost feel the 'paleo me' crawling out of the surf millions, or is it billions, of years ago. It makes me feel connected, to everything."

"Me, too," she said. "I think if God designed churches, He'd just have all the services here on the beach or in the forest."

"Probably. And I think He'd be partial to beaches like this one with carnival rides in the background. Hey, want to have some fun?" I asked.

"Doing what?"

"Only my favorite thing at the Santa Cruz boardwalk: riding the hundred-year-old wooden roller coaster. I hear almost everyone makes it back alive. By the way, that last part was a joke. See the red 'K' on my imaginary T-shirt?"

"Okay. I'd like that."

Roller coasters are by their nature, erotic. Designed for two people per car. Thrown together. Adrenaline rushes. Peaks and valleys. The anticipation, the turning loose, giving up all control before the plunge.

It wasn't a formal date, but we were closer after we wobbled off the platform at the end of the ride. On the walk back to where we were staying, I told her that I had enjoyed meeting her and sideways mentioned that my dropping her off at her home the next afternoon wouldn't be out of my way if her mom could manage to drive herself back over the Santa Cruz mountains to Mountain View.

She said she'd talk to her mom and let me know. I don't remember if we held hands, but I know I didn't kiss her goodnight. It wasn't time for that yet, or I was too shy.

Somewhere on the beach that evening, though, the last little chunk of my old faith armor dropped into the sand and was washed away by the waves.

I never heard it fall.

The next morning, we ended the retreat by celebrating Eucharist on the beach as before. For some reason I kept seeing an image in my head of Jesus hanging on a cross made of roses. Alice said she could make it home by herself and Laura joined me in my beat-up yellow VW bug. Laura had persuaded her mother to sell the house and move to a fancy apartment complex. When I dropped her off, I mentioned that I'd be at the next Christian Community gathering the following week. She said she might see me there.

And she did. The next time I saw her, it was at the regular Christian Community weekly meeting. I was driving my brother's hotrod pickup truck.

"There's a full moon tonight. Would you like to drive out the beach after the meeting is over?"

"Sure," she replied.

We must have been overheard about going to the beach because, as we are getting into my truck, Claire, the manhunter, showed up at the door and asked if she could come along. That wasn't in my plans, but I didn't quite know what to say. She joined us. The three of us squeezed onto the bench seat of the old pickup as I took the back roads out to Pescadero. Claire even tried to sit between me and Laura on my beach blanket, but we prevented that. What I'd planned for a romantic evening got short-circuited, and it was a quick trip out and back. I dropped Claire off and took Laura home. Uncharacteristically assertive for her, Laura said, "If you'd dropped me off first, that would have been the end of it." I got the message.

The next ten days I was operating my food concession trailer at the San Joaquin County Fair in Stockton. I must have made a dozen trips to the phone booth, dialing Laura's number several times, and hanging up before I got up the courage to ask her out on the first real date of my life. I took her to San Francisco to a nice restaurant and then to see a play. On our way back, the car stalled at a red light, not because of a mechanical problem but because of a long and deep first kiss.

That kiss paled compared to the next one. It was my year for retreats as well as love. I'd gotten myself involved with some other Protestants, the Young Life Organization, and had been helping them with fundraising. I had been scheduled to attend one of their retreats up in the Sierra foothills in late August and asked if Laura could come along.

We had a whole weekend together, subtracting the separate sleeping arrangements the camp insisted on. I remember sitting on a log, felled as a small bridge. We sat on that log and kissed for a good ten minutes without coming up for air. It's surprising we didn't fall over backwards into the creek.

But I was falling somewhere. I was falling in love. This was not according to plan. I had planned to sow some wild oats, have a fling, a few one-night stands, love 'em and leave 'em. And now, it was beginning to feel like it was with Amy. Laura was different: shyer, more reserved. Now, I was the chaser, not the chased; and Laura was the chased, but not as chaste as Amy. But the feelings were eerily similar.

"Damnit, God. This wasn't our deal. It's too soon. I told you I'd get ordained first, and then, if I met a woman... Why now? Why couldn't you have let me have my fling, my good time. I think I deserve it. I've been pretty good, done what you wanted."

God kept His mouth shut.

By the time Laura was ready to return to school in Portland the following month, we had spent a good deal of time together. I knew I was getting in deep, way past my safety point. My European travel plans were still only on paper and were far from my mind. As soon as I put Laura on the plane to school, I already missed her.

Yet, God was still calling. But what was He saying? How could he want me to be a celibate priest and then give me this woman as a gift? It may seem a strange, even ridiculous dilemma to someone who has never found themselves exactly here. But that's how I felt.

I struggled with this the first month Laura was in school. Finally, I knew what I had to do: what I had always believed I was called to do. I was in too deep to just make a phone call, so I arranged to fly up to Portland—only my second plane trip ever—to spend the weekend with her. I would let her down easy.

We had a wonderful weekend together. I met her friends; we soaked in a Japanese tub; we shared meals. One night she spent two hours just taking my socks off. She showed me the window where she'd dropped the rose petals. Because she was in a dorm, we didn't sleep together. And then it was Sunday afternoon, and I was to leave the next morning.

And I still hadn't told her why I had really come to see her. My stomach was tied in knots. So was my heart. I had to tell her. I just had to find a way. Goddammit, I had to get back on that plane in the morning and go back to my life, to my planned bacchanal, to the priesthood, to celibacy.

Just before dinner on Sunday evening, we joined the campus ministry group for a prayer service. I can no longer picture where we met or anything of the service itself. For some reason Laura and I were sitting on the floor, our knees bent towards our chests and our backs resting against a brick wall. Sitting there with my eyes closed, I was suddenly aware of knowing, *"What if you could be a priest and be married too."*

I didn't hear this, experience it as a voice, either from inside or outside myself. I didn't see it either, like a vision in my mind's eye. It didn't seem like it was God talking. It was more like I felt it, I *felt* the words, the sentence. I felt myself *inside* the sentence, like it wrapped itself around me, like it was alive, a power outside of me, around me.

It took me away from myself, all other sensation, all memory. It was as though I was in my own personal "black hole" spinning round in its own universe. Nothing else except those felt words could get in or out.

The sensation lasted for several days, two, three—half a week? I remember nothing from that moment until I found myself in the living room of Jim Pogge's apartment in San Jose a few days later.

I know that the service must have ended, that we must have had dinner, that I must have spent another night on the couch in Laura's dorm common room. I must have kissed her goodbye the next morning, gotten across town to the airport and flown back to California. Which airport? San Jose, probably, but I have no memory of it. I don't know what I did for a car, what else I did, or where I slept during those next several days I spent in my black hole.

Eventually, I found myself in Jim Pogge's living room, and memory started to kick in again. I must have called Jim and asked to come see him. Jim was a former professor in the seminary, an ex-priest who had left and married a nun he had worked with in a ministry to San Jose's Latino community. They were what might be called the Church's "Power Couple" if such a thing existed: deeply in love with one another, with the church, and with the people they served.

"Fr. Jim, I don't know what to do. I feel called by God to be a priest, but I love this woman. It's almost like God has also given me this relationship as a gift."

"I'm not your dad, and I'm not officially a priest anymore. There's no need to call me 'Father.' Jim will do."

"Okay, Fa... I mean Jim. But is there any way you can help me figure out the right thing to do? I went through this before and stayed in the seminary but this time, I don't know."

"Nove, you know I can't make your decision for you. All I can really do is tell you how it is for me. I do agree with you and what you've told me about Ed Miller's advice. He's wrong, as far as I'm concerned. I wouldn't say that God gives us the gift of celibacy and I certainly no longer believe that celibacy and the priesthood are meant to go hand in hand.

"When Pat and I met, we were both doing what we believed God wanted us to do. We both felt 'called,' she as much as me. But it doesn't feel wrong to be together either. It feels more *right* than anything I've ever done. And I know Pat feels the same way."

"But what about God? What does He think?"

"The mind of God? You want me to read that?"

"No. Not really, I guess, but I have to find some way to figure this out. I've known a lot of guys who left the seminary over the years. Most of those who entered the seminary, in fact, have left. But they all decided that they didn't want to be a priest or that God wasn't really calling them. That's kind of what Ed Miller said. No celibacy, no calling, no priesthood.

"But I still feel 'called.' It's not like I want to leave. But there is another part of me that also feels called, to have a partner in life, a wife, maybe even children, a family. And both calls seem to be coming from the same place. From inside me? From God? I can't tell anymore. I just know they both come from the same place and they're both real. They both touch the core of who I am, my soul."

Jim looked across the room at me. "Again, all I can tell you, Nove, is how it's been for me. I did get ordained. I was a priest for many years. And now, they tell me I'm not. But I'm still me, the same person, still trying to live the life and values I always have. Am I still a priest *and* married? The church says no. But that's just a label. True, things are different, better in most ways. But they're also still the same.

People speak of faith as though it were a certainty, as

though you can prove it, like the medieval theologians with their various 'proofs' for the existence of God. But it's not like that. It's a belief, a conviction. It involves the risk of being wrong, taking a chance.

Pat and I acted on faith when we chose to be together. It contradicted everything we had been taught about being a priest or a nun. We acted on our faith, took a risk, and we're glad we did. What does God think about what we're doing? We think He, or maybe She, approves, but you'll have to ask that of God yourself."

Jim and Pat provided no easy answer for me—no answer at all other than their own lives. I did leave with a clearer sense of direction. I knew that I had a choice—either give up Laura or take a leap of faith.

Two days later, after eight years in the seminary and a lifetime of wanting to be a priest, I called a woman on the phone that I had known less than three months and asked her to marry me. She immediately said *yes* seven times.

PART V

AFTER THE FALL

A WOMAN SCORNED

Until the day I told my mother that I had decided to marry Laura instead of becoming a Catholic priest, I'd believed that my decision to be a priest was mine alone—well, mine and God's. I knew that my mother was happy about the priest plan; any Catholic mother would have been. I suppose the signs were there—her buying me the chalice, bragging to her friends about me, getting involved in seminary fundraisers—though up until that moment, I had been going blissfully along, thinking that my life was my own to live.

The Roman Catholic Church is the most hierarchical of organizations. Supposedly, God Himself is at the top. Then you've got the pope, the cardinals, archbishops, bishops, abbots, monsignors, priests, seminarians, laymen, and altar boys. At the very bottom, bearing the weight of this enormous pyramid, are women. If a woman wants to improve her chances of getting past the servant's quarters in heaven, her options are limited. Mary's singular opportunity of giving birth to the Good Lord Himself was a one-time deal. Getting martyred helps, provided one is still a virgin. Or, a woman can follow Shakespeare's advice and "get thee to a nunnery." But for the average Catholic woman, her best chance is for her son to become a priest.

If a Catholic mother's son becomes a priest, it's like a first-class ticket to heaven. And, even before the train leaves for the pearly gates, life is good. Perhaps the best part, never spoken, is that she doesn't have to share her boy with that "other woman," a wife. Even though he's dedicated his life to God, he's still all hers. If she has other children to produce grand-kids, then it just doesn't get any better.

So, understandably, I was nervous. After eight years in the seminary, getting married was no less news to me than any-one else; so, I knew it would come as a shock to my parents. I'd expected that it would elicit a response from my mother stronger than mild surprise. Before dinner, one of my younger brothers had told me that he was dropping out of college and moving in with his girlfriend. He was concerned about Moth-er's reaction, but I told him to relax. "Don't worry," I assured him. "After she hears what I have to say, she won't care or ev-en remember."

After dinner that evening, I'd asked my parents to sit at the kitchen table, as I had something that I wanted to tell them.

"I've decided to marry Laura," I managed to blurt out. "I asked her to marry me, and she said yes. We're getting mar-ried in the spring."

My dad didn't say anything right then. He was probably thinking that his son had finally come to his senses, while knowing that the shit was about to hit the fan from my mother's side of the table, and a lot of it would get sprayed on him. Later, his counsel was to delay our wedding plans for a while, which turned out to be good advice. He liked Laura, and I think that my becoming more "regular" made us a little closer.

Mother's face, though, became Mt. Rushmore—before the carving had started. I know she must have said at least something that night, but I've blotted it out.

A few days later she had me meet her at a local restaurant not far from her house. In the late afternoon we had the dimly lit back section of the restaurant to ourselves. I'm not certain that every single word related here was said that very afternoon or spread out over the next few months, but my memory locates it here.

"I guess you know I'm going to hell now," she began. "I've done a lot of bad things in my life, but when you decided to become a priest, I truly believed that it meant God had forgiven me."

Define *bad*. It's not just that they had broken the mold when God made my mother, but I think her creation is what triggered that phrase in the first place. Her behavior constituted its own category. Still, I was not prepared for what I heard next.

"I think I've told you before that I was married, briefly, to my cousin."

Well, no, not exactly. I'd known that both her parents had died during the Depression when she was just sixteen. Her older brother had gotten the insurance check and had taken off—leaving her with two younger siblings, aged two and four. "What's a girl to do?" she always used to ask, telling us the story of how she'd opened a little tavern, a honky-tonk she called it, on the outskirts of Austin, Texas, to support herself and her siblings. So, there she was, selling beer to the CCC boys before she was legally old enough to drink herself. She'd called the place Bella Vista.

"Clyde came out to Bella Vista," she explained. "He was several years older than me and hadn't seen me since I was a kid on the ranch. And suddenly, he was taken with me—I was a cutie—and wanted me to marry him. Of course, I told him 'no way.' He wasn't bad-looking and was nice and all, but we were cousins, *first* cousins. Still, he kept pestering me, and I kept saying no."

"Bella Vista was just getting started, and we weren't making hardly any money yet. I was boarding my little siblings, Bonnie and Rusty, in town and trying to keep them in school. When I fell behind in their 'keep' the landlady threatened to kick them out and the school people were making threats about taking them away from me. They were my siblings; more like my kids and the only thing I had left from my parents. But I was a single woman, just eighteen myself, and I was in the beer business. This is when Clyde came back around and switched his tactics."

She looked at me hard and kept going.

"'Mac,' he told me, 'if you marry me, I can support us, and we can keep the kids. You can stay home and take care of 'em. And we don't have to 'do' anything if you don't want to.'

"It worked. I was getting desperate to save my kids, and I agreed to marry him, though not in a Catholic Church."

My mother married her own first cousin? Before my dad? Seriously? But then it got better. Actually, worse. Much worse.

"So, we got married. But then Clyde changed his tune. He wanted me to 'sleep with him' and told me that as his wife I was obligated to do so. I refused. I just couldn't do it. It was wrong, even to save the kids. We were standing in the little cabin that I had built for myself on the creek, right next to Bella Vista. Clyde went to the bedside table and pulled out the silver-handled pistol that my Daddy had given me to protect myself. He pointed the gun at me and yelled, 'If I can't have you, nobody can.' He missed, twice, before turning the gun on himself and pulling the trigger.

"I screamed, and my helper came running from the bar. We carried Clyde out to the middle of Bull Creek Road and flagged down a passing car. We got him to the hospital, where he lived for three more days. The sheriff came and questioned me, but Clyde insisted that he had shot himself. I was grateful for that, and I agreed to lie in his hospital bed and hold him while a priest came in and married us in the Church."

Although that was how Mother told the story that day, I overheard her later tell a different version to someone else. In that story there was a struggle over the gun. It was unclear whose hand had held it. Three shots were still fired, all into Clyde's torso—an unlikely suicide scenario. It's no great surprise that the sheriff had had his suspicions.

Murder? Perhaps. Self-defense? Quite possibly. Either way, Clyde died.

I listened silently, watching Mother's face. Now, that I wasn't going to be a priest anymore I was starting to hear confessions—my own mother's—but I had no words to absolve her from her ghosts.

Forget the priesthood. Forget getting married. I was sitting there realizing that I'd always been just a couple of small caliber bullets away from not being here at all. Talk about your "what ifs." I had thought that when Mother had said she was going to hell, she was using hyperbole to push me in her direction, to make me feel sorry for her. But she had probably meant it literally. She'd probably killed a man—her first cousin—after marrying him under questionable circumstancees, and it had been hanging on her conscience ever since before I'd been me. Which I wouldn't have ever been if one of those shots in that little cabin had found a different mark.

While this revelation was starting to sink in, Mother just kept pushing onward breaking all the bounds.

"You know you're not my first son," she went on. "I had another with a man I didn't love, before your daddy."

I'd had a vague childhood memory of an older boy living with us for a time. But I didn't know why. Now she was telling me that he was my *brother*?

"I used that man's credit to get a loan to rebuild my bar after it burned down. Well, after my friend Virginia and I burnt it down. Once the first Bella Vista had gotten to making some money a couple who were working for me—turns out they were ex-cons—took over my business. They forced me to move into Austin and threatened to kill me if I wasn't satisfied with the ten dollars a week rent, they were going to pay me. The kids and I couldn't survive on that.

"The only way to get rid of them was to burn the place down. So, one night, Virginia and I borrowed her mother's car and drove out from Austin. We parked about a mile away and waited until after midnight when I knew the place would be closed. We took some newspaper and a jar of coal-oil [kerosene] and snuck down to the bar. We crumpled up the paper and stuffed it under the front steps, poured the coal-oil over it and set it on fire.

"We got out of there before anybody saw us. The sheriff had his suspicions and grilled me twice but never tried to arrest me. I got the insurance money, but it wasn't enough to rebuild. And, in those days, the banks wouldn't loan money to a single woman. So that's why I married Billy, but I never planned to have a child with him. Birth control not being what it is today; that plan didn't work. And that's when your older brother came along.

"I never loved Troy. I couldn't. The nurses at the hospital were surprised at my reaction to my baby and assured me that I would get used to him. But I didn't. He reminded me of his father Billy—that 'momma's boy' who kept living with his mother and was afraid to even tell her he'd married me. Your brother reminded me of what I had done, my sin, which reminded me of all my other sins. Later, after I moved to California to help with the war effort, I found Troy some foster parents; boring like Billy, but they took good care of him.

"But 'My Love'—your daddy—wanted him, or at least thought we should do the right thing. When he got back from the War, he insisted that we take Troy back. I tried. I really tried. But when you were born, and your brothers started coming along, I just couldn't do it. I insisted that we send him away. I don't think your daddy has ever forgiven me. And now, I don't know that God has either."

As mother told the story, I could see the pain in her face. She wasn't sitting in a restaurant with me in 1971. She was reliving her history from more than thirty years before, baring her soul—to me, to God, to herself.

I guess I should have been shocked. It would have been a normal reaction to suddenly learning that one had an older brother. But I wasn't. This was the mother whose behavior I'd gotten used to in my twenty-two years on the planet. This was the same mother I'd found burning counterfeit money in our garage when I was six. It was the mother who'd put me on an untrained elephant when I was eight to see if it would be safe for other children—the same mother who gave me the keys to a barely running station wagon, filled with screaming cousins and siblings, and told me to drive them home, one hundred and fifty miles away, before I had a driver's license. And that's all just for starters.

So, no, I wasn't shocked—not even about the abortion that she didn't quite admit to, though I could piece it together.

That was back in 1942, as my dad was leaving for war.

When a man goes to war, he doesn't know if he'll return. When my father left for the Pacific in 1942, he was leaving behind a young bride of only a few months; a young bride with three mouths to feed; her own toddler son, and two budding teenagers left her by her deceased parents. The last thing she needed was one more little person to care for, especially if her husband failed to return.

Maybe they should have been more careful, but it was a lot harder in those pre-pill days. Just before boarding the troop ship, he'd insisted that she get rid of the child they'd conceived, just months into their marriage. He had it arranged; and she, strong-willed, independent woman though she was, was still his obedient wife. And he was right. One more child would have been at least one too many. But it would have been her first-born, at least the first-born with a man she loved. She did what she was told, but she never forgave him. And God must not have forgiven them either because the marriage was child-less for almost nine years. The first four were understandable because thousands of miles of ocean separated them but even when Dad returned there was no baby for her to hold and see the reflection of her husband in her arms.

Until I came along. And then the floodgates opened: four sons in five years. Another one four years later. And finally, a daughter.

So now, in the space of an hour, I'd gone from being her oldest child to having two older siblings, one dead and one missing in action. *What else did mother have to spring on me? How many other sins did my priestly plans cover up? Did I even want to know?*

I took a sip of my nearly cold coffee, wishing now that I'd ordered a scotch and soda, a double.

A phrase always at the ready on my mother's lips was, "You didn't live through the Depression." I didn't, but I've read *Grapes of Wrath, The Worst Hard Times,* and enough other Depression and Dust Bowl stories to have a fairly good idea of how bad it was. But what I heard, whenever she opined about the '30s, was about the poverty and the loss of physical things.

Until 1929 she had enjoyed a somewhat privileged, if quirky, life. Growing up on a circus, performing to the adula-tion of the roaring crowds, and life on a five-hundred-acre ranch in the off-season held happy memories. While this was offset by being teased by other kids (probably jealous) for be-ing on a circus and having to be farmed out to local families so she could attend school, it was the life she relived in her dreams.

But the Depression had ended all that. The circus quickly failed. Her daddy had to work harder and be away from the family more. She was likely an unwilling secret-keeper to her mother's infidelity.

Her brief diary of a final journey with her dying father, seeking help from the brother who had managed to enrich himself from the family's misfortunes, is heart-wrenching. Having been evicted from his brother's home because of fear of contagion of his tuberculosis, he'd died on the road and was buried in the rain on the Alabama border. A few months later, he was followed in death by his much younger wife, also from tuberculosis as well as a broken heart. My mother's inheritance, then, was her younger siblings.

I don't know how much of this I specifically heard that day in that restaurant, but it was all there, in one form or another. The Depression that "you didn't live through" did not simply deprive her of material goods. It took her parents, her youth, and a good part of her soul.

There were other things, both spoken and hinted at.

I never met the man my mother had started to fall in love with the day he'd tied his horse to the post of her little cabin and almost pulled it down. When my dad came back from the War, he'd returned a different, sadder, man. In the too-short twenty-five years that I knew him, he never spoke about the war—never said a single word. He had been "fighting the Japs" in the Pacific, as they said in those days. He'd seen things a man shouldn't have to see and had done things a man shouldn't have to do.

My mother, however, was ready to party. She'd helped with the war effort on the home front, working as a welder at Kaiser shipyards. But now the war was over. Her grief over the loss of her parents had subsided; her siblings were almost raised; and she had freed herself, temporarily at least, of her own young son. A male co-worker at the nightclub where she was now a photographer had skipped the war. He had no war injuries, physical or emotional, and he liked Mother. Neither that day, nor any other, did she ever admit to anything inappropriate, but just after my dad died, she called that man. She told me that he'd said, "Mac, what took you so long?" and hung up the phone. So, we'll never know if there was yet another sin that she felt that God had overlooked after I joined the seminary.

But my being called to the priesthood washed away all her real and imagined sins and made her right with God.

And now what?

There was really nothing I could say. Oh, I could spiel off some of my theology about God's universal forgiveness. But she already knew that, having been Catholic longer than I, and it wasn't taking. I didn't buy her guilt trip and wasn't going to play that game. She wasn't going to hell, and even if she were, it wasn't because of my decision not to be a priest. And I sure as hell wasn't going to try to convince her that she wasn't losing me to another woman.

I probably told her I would think about what she had said. And I did. Still am.

What I thought, and think, mostly about, was how fortunate I was to have presented my mother with a fait accompli. When I told her that I was getting married and ending my studies for the priesthood I was already engaged. Had I just told Mother that I was thinking about getting married? Or, God forbid, asked for her opinion I might never have had the stamina or courage to follow through.

I realized that, until this moment, I had never disappointed my mother. It wasn't that I'd tried to please her, at least not that I was aware. Not at all. It's just that I always had. She was happy with everything I did. After all, I was her salvation. She was overjoyed that I was going to be a priest. And my getting a summer job on a carnival provided her with an opportunity to "rejoin the circus" and recapture her youth. Within just a couple of weeks after I started selling amusement ride tickets the summer after sophomore year, she, my aunt, and several siblings and cousins were also traveling with the show. Her reverence for Larry, the owner, was not unlike what she expressed about her circus-owner daddy. And, when I started my own business, first selling balloons and snow cones at parades and eventually getting some kiddie rides and trying to go into the carnival business myself, the return to the wonderful circus years, before the Depression was almost complete.

I had never thought of myself as a "momma's boy" clinging to my mother, seeking her approval. After all, I'd left home at thirteen, living at the seminary for nine months a year. But, unrecognized by me, my plans for myself, coincided with hers for me. I did everything she wanted, without even knowing it. Looking back, I can recall several times her taking me into her confidence, sharing secrets one should discuss with a spouse, not one's child.

She didn't give up, and kept finding reasons for me to question my decision—smaller ones, like short-comings in Laura, or how would I make a living. Or what it would do to our family business? When none of that worked, she'd switched tactics. She introduced me to someone else. I guess she figured that if her son was getting married, leaving her for another woman, it should at least be someone of whom she approved. But that day in the restaurant was the day she gave it her best shot, pulled out the stops, tried to get God involved.

Nothing worked. I didn't become a priest. I did get married.

And, apart from Mother, most people were happy about my decision, especially my children, for whom my choice had definite existential consequences, their own *"what if."*

Mother lived for almost forty more years. After my dad's death, she spent the last thirty years of her life as a celibate herself.

WHAT NOW

I had taken a risk, made the leap of faith. And when I landed, I was in unfamiliar territory, like I had parachuted into a foreign land without a map: with no understanding of the language, geography, or culture. For nearly all of it, my life had been going in only one direction—two if you counted the circus. That voice, or whatever it was that had wrapped me inside itself with the words, or feeling, *"What if you can be a priest and married too?"* wasn't offering any further instructions. *How was I to live my life? What was I supposed to do to support myself? How was I still to understand the "call" I had felt since second grade?*

I tried to get back into the seminary. One of the changes instituted by the Vatican II Council was the restoration of the "permanent diaconate." This was like playing in the minor leagues. Men—married men—could now become deacons, kind of junior varsity priests. They couldn't say Mass or hear confessions, but they could baptize, preach sermons, and help at funerals. There were a couple of gotchas. No pay, as it was all volunteer. And, you had to be at least thirty-five years old, whereas I was just twenty-two. Yes, you could be married. But as part of the vows you took, you had to promise that, if you were fortunate enough to have your wife die on you, you would not remarry. Of course, you could then become a priest, so there was that.

I thought, *"Well maybe someday I'll want to be a deacon, so as long as the opportunity is available, I may as well go ahead and finish my theological education."* And, who knew, as fast as the Church had been changing in the last few years, they might soon start ordaining married men to the priesthood. I'm not saying it was a good plan. It didn't really address more immediate concerns such as food, rent, etc., but it was a plan.

So, I went over to Menlo Park to St. Patrick's Theologate. I met with the rector Fr. Farrell and told him my plan.

He told me his.

"No."

My dad had persuaded Laura and me to delay our wedding from the coming spring. "Take a little time," he advised. "This whole marriage thing is so new to you."

As a temporary fix, I headed East. Laura was still up in Portland in college, and I really had nothing on my agenda. According to my previous plan, I was to be in Europe, seeing the sights of the ancient world and enjoying the pleasures of its young ladies. But now, being engaged, that would probably be in poor taste.

I'd heard California congressman Pete McCloskey speak at Stanford University. He was an ex-marine and shared most young people's opinions on the Vietnam War. He was about to undertake a quixotic quest to try to do to Richard Nixon in the New Hampshire presidential primary what Eugene McCarthy had done to Lyndon Johnson four years before. And he was looking for volunteers to join him. I signed up.

The various "clunkers" I'd been driving for the last several years begged me not to force them to try to make the trip all the way to the other side of the country. So, I bought my first new car three days before I left: a Datsun B-210 coupe, royal blue. It didn't set particularly well with Laura, as I hadn't bought her an engagement ring yet. But in fairness, given my previous history, the value of cars I understood; tiny, over-priced pieces of rock, not so much.

My third brother down (Bull) had been having a bit of trouble with Dad. I had recently interrupted a fight between him and Dad one day. When I'd found out where the yelling was coming from, he was taunting his "old man" to "go ahead and shoot me, if you got the guts" as our dad stood with his .22 pistol in his hand. They were having a disagreement about Dad having taken his keys away and his having smashed the car windows with a sledgehammer in retaliation. Foolishly, I placed myself between the two of them, in a direct line of fire, and started talking. But, "all's well, that ends well." I persuad-ed Dad to let me hold the gun for safekeeping and told my brother he owed Dad an apology. I won't say that ended the war, but at least a truce was called that day before blood was spilled. Another one of those damned *what ifs*.

I decided that, to keep my brother alive (and Dad out of jail), I would invite him to come along and share the driving, at least as far as some of our relatives, where he could stay for a while.

We took a side trip through the South to catch a cousin's wedding and stopped at a Mexican border town to get some souvenirs. Even then, switchblades were illegal in "el Norte," but my brother picked up a couple anyway. We walked across, did some shopping, and had a few *cervezas*. It was dark as we walked back through U.S. immigration. His feet had gotten sore from his cool but uncomfortable cowboy boots, so he took them off and stuck the switchblades inside. I pulled out my ID and breezed through security much less rigorous than what we face after 9/11.

I looked back to see my dark-complexioned brother— getting lighter as he got older, but still browner than some of the Mexicans—talking to the customs officer barefoot, boots in hand as if he were getting ready to wade the Rio Grande.

"What country are you from, son?" the officer asked.

Smart-assed as always, he pointed to the U.S. side and said, "That one." A half-hour later, he finally got back across. The switchblades did not.

My trip ended in Keene in southwestern New Hampshire, where I staffed a little office during the week and coordinated the volunteers for weekend doorbelling. On Friday nights I usually went to a couple of local (in my West Coast mind) colleges, which were spread over two of those tiny states they have back there. It was a hundred-mile round trip. It would have been the perfect setup; if I weren't engaged. The colleges were all women's institutions: Mt. Holyoke, Smith, and the like.

My biggest temptation came from the "enemy" camp. Pete McCloskey was then still a Republican, and he was trying to unseat Richard Nixon in the Republican primary. But Ed Muskie was the Democrat who, everyone then expected, to be the Democratic nominee in the fall. As a Democrat myself, and needing some social life during the week, I went to as many Democratic events as Republican ones.

I didn't exactly "sleep with the enemy," but there was a young woman, a Muskie volunteer named Pam who lived in town and took a liking to me. And the real enemy, the mutual one, was always "tricky Dick" Nixon. Pam knew I was engaged but probably would have overlooked that technicality had I found myself willing to do so. I mean, seriously, do the "rules of engagement" extend all the way across the country? Maybe, had I not had so much invested in my particular engagement, leaving the priesthood and all, I may have more seriously considered seeing where my friendship with Pam would take me. But I didn't. *What if?*

Despite a lot of tromping through the snow and the ungodly mud they euphemistically call the "Spring Melt," we lost. Pulling a little under twenty percent of the vote, our effort proved a mere pimple on Nixon's behind. I said goodbye to all the ladies I'd met, retrieved my brother, and headed home.

When I got home a letter awaited me. It came to my parents' house, which was still my official address. The return address indicated that it was from the local draft board. Dad even recognized some of the names in the signature block; not that it mattered. The letter informed me that I had been reclassified 1-A and that I was to report in ten days to the induction center in Oakland for a pre-induction physical. I'm sure my mother was at least thinking, "See. I told you so," but, to her credit, she kept her actual mouth shut.

Fuck. Double fuck. I'd been classified 4-D ever since I'd gotten my draft card and didn't remember ever giving my draft status a thought when I decided to get married. The draft and the war pissed me off, and I had done my share of protesting, but it had always been on somebody else's behalf. I had never considered personally facing these realities. That's how insulated we were in the seminary.

What had happened? I had requested a leave of absence from the seminary before I graduated college. I explained to the priest who was the new Sacramento Vocations Director that I just needed a year off, that I fully intended to return to the seminary the following year to complete my studies and get ordained. That was before I met Laura, but there was no way he knew about that, I didn't think.

Did he fail to process my request? Maybe Fr. Farrell had told him of my visit and he then ratted me out to the draft board. Or maybe Nixon didn't like people campaigning against him in New Hampshire and changed my status on his own.

It was surreal. The ticket for the bus that left the Fairfield station just before dawn was free. And it was round trip, so I knew there were no plans to ship me off that very day. I took a seat towards the back and sat down, thinking I could at least finish my night's sleep. But, of course, that was impossible.

Between contemplating my own fate and looking around the bus, wondering how many of the faces on that bus would still be attached to their owners in five years, two, or even one, I felt all the potholes the bus hit on the way to Oakland, an hour away.

We got there about daybreak and filed into the most antiseptically sterile building I've ever had the misfortune to encounter. Mostly what I remember were lines on the floor: red, green, yellow, white, going this way and that, directing us ever closer to the jungles of Vietnam. We had to constantly look down to get anywhere, which was just as well since nobody felt like looking up anyway. Most of the young men felt lost, disoriented, and hopeless.

As we moved along the lines, making right and left turns as ordered, it seemed like we lost progressively more of our clothing as if they were already starting to strip us of our dignity, our personality, our humanity. The last piece came off, our drawers, just before the "grab and cough." If you got through the feet, eyes, ears, and tooth test, the final exam was to be put in a room with everybody else, buck naked, where they grabbed your junk and told you to cough. Unfortunately, I passed.

In the afternoon, we sat down to fill out paperwork and take an IQ test. The only good part was that we got our clothes back. I thought about purposely trying to flunk the test, but decided it wasn't worth the effort. When I got home, about nightfall, Dad picked me up at the bus station.

All in all, it was about the most dehumanizing experience of my life, except possibly the Little Bill incident, but I guess I'm lucky because there are lots worse things that can happen to people.

A few days later the recruiters started calling: The Marines, Navy, Air Force, but not the Coast Guard. Apparently, I'd "aced" the intelligence test.

"You're officer material," they told me. "You don't want to

go to 'Nam and get shot up." This from the armed forces re-cruiters. They didn't actually say I *wouldn't* go to 'Nam but held out hope that, if I signed up for officer training, life would be better. They reminded me of Jack Kent's "flatties" on the carnival.

By this time, everyone knew the Vietnam War was wrong, morally, and in every other way. Even Richard Nixon knew it was wrong. His campaign to end it was what got him elected. But he kept it going because he had to save face. Not the hun-dred or so young faces a week that were still coming back to Travis Air Force Base in body bags, but his own, or the coun-try's, or God's, or some goddamn face somewhere.

After thinking about it, and not too long, I decided to apply for CO, conscientious objector status. This could still get me sent to Vietnam, but at least I wouldn't have to shoot at people. If I was lucky, I might get something stateside, something saf-er, like working in the projects in South Chicago. I figured it would be a slam dunk, with my seminary background and all. I got the paperwork, began filling it out and started searching for people to provide the required reference letters to prove that I wasn't just being a chicken and secretly enjoyed—having other people—kill gooks.

I went to the priest who had taught me how to think in theology class, to question, to dig deeper, to get behind the rules, and ask that simple question, *"What would Jesus do?"* in theologically more nuanced language, of course.

Triple fuck. The bastard wouldn't do it, wouldn't write me a letter, wouldn't even sign one if I wrote it myself. Something about the Catholic Church's "Just War" theory, which would hardly apply to Vietnam in any case. Or maybe it was his way of saying, "See, I told you so," for leaving the seminary.

I did manage to get enough letters and sent the package off. There were a few requests for clarification, more docu-mentation, and then nothing for months. The process dragged on for over a year. Then one day, after I was already married and had been checking out retirement communities in Canada, I got a letter. It mentioned nothing about my request for conscientious objector status. It simply stated that I had been re-classified by the selective service system into a category I had never heard of. The classification was "1-H, holding". Maybe it just meant "pain in the ass." And I guess that's where I still am—holding. So, if there's ever a war where they need geriatric soldiers, I'm their man.

Certainly, had I managed to get myself killed in Vietnam, or even South Chicago, that would have solved my dilemma. But I didn't, so I was still at a loss as to where to go in life.

Even if I was no longer going to be able to transform bread into Jesus's body, I could still transform sugar into cotton candy. But Mother was already lobbying, pushing me out, wanting my share of the business for another brother. It seemed that giving up the priesthood had also meant giving up the circus.

I looked in the mirror and saw that six-year-old in church listening to God talking to Fr. Murphy. I saw the gung-ho Catholic schoolboy in his proper uniform slurping up what the nuns were dishing out. I saw the young seminarian practically crouching under his desk like he was practicing an atomic bomb drill as Fr. Luke re-arranged the priesthood. I saw a teenage carnie/seminarian starting to learn about the compromise that real life entailed. I saw a college student beginning to open the Book of Questions. I saw the man who took a leap of faith for the woman he loved. But when I looked for me now, the mirror fogged over, leaving a ghost of an image.

Clearly, the road forward was going to be anything but clear.

EPILOGUE

I was sitting in a pizza joint having a mug of brew and a slice or two with a couple of other seminarians and one of our professors. None of us were wearing Roman collars, and I wasn't aware that we were talking religion. A stranger approached our table, a young man. He addressed the priest. "You're a priest, right? Well, when I was a kid, I was baptized Catholic, but I don't want to be one anymore. How do you get out of that organization?"

We were mute, including the priest. Truth is, there's no official way to become completely un-Catholic. You can manage to get yourself excommunicated, but that just means you're no longer allowed to take communion. Baptism, the church teaches, puts an indelible mark on your soul. It's the same way with being a priest. Holy Orders—getting ordained—is another of the Catholic Church's sacraments that is not repeatable or removable—that indelible mark again. And I don't think you can get away from it even if you only just come close. It's in your blood, your way of looking at life. Regardless of what path your life takes, it's still there.

After I got married, I worked for the Catholic Church for

nearly twenty years as a lay minister. Even after I went on to focus on business, I've never forgotten that encounter with the young woman in the Santa Cruz mountains, "Nove, you're going to make a good priest." Whatever that means, in its myriad forms, I've tried to live my life that way: never succeeding, rarely even coming close, but still trying.

I did eventually part company with the official Roman Catholic Church for some personal and theological reasons but mainly because of its inherent sexism and its corporate cover-up of its personnel's abuse of children. To my mind, that is the true sacrilege, the unforgivable sin.

***

And the circus, how do you run away from that?

On May 21, 2017, Ringling Brothers, Barnum & Bailey Combined Shows—*The Greatest Show on Earth*—offered its last performance on Long Island, New York, effectively ending more than two centuries of tradition, the American traveling circus. A year earlier, the show had retired its last elephants after years of pressure from animal rights activists. There are a few traveling shows still touring, but the handwriting is on the tent walls. Pachyderms, clowns, and trapeze artists have been replaced by YouTube, Facebook, and Twitter. In effect, the whole world has run away from the circus.

But looked at a different way, the circus is more than what ended with that last Ringling Brothers performance. It's something you're born to. Even if they transfused all my blood, somehow circus blood would still be flowing through my veins. It's not just three rings and performances, but a way of looking at life, a way of living life.

Or, as Mother always said, "Take a chance."

ACKNOWLEDGEMENTS
ONE LAST CONFESSION AND SOME THANKSGIVINGS

I take full responsibility for the memories contained herein. Now that doesn't mean that each and every one of them corresponds to objective reality or that other's memories may not differ. I'm not a tape recorder or a video camera, and I've also changed a few names along the way to protect the innocent and the guilty.

As to the origin of my writing skills, or lack thereof, that is a split decision. The early money goes on my late mother. While the only thing she ever had published was a partial letter in Andrew Carrol's anthology, *War Letters: Extraordinary Correspondence from American Wars,* her output included two thousand of those war letters to my dad along with a two-hundred-page monograph about her early life experiences. On the other hand, perhaps writing genetics works backwards and I inherited whatever talent I have from my daughter, Dr. Susan V. Meyers, professor of English at Seattle University. In either case, thanks.

Thanks also to all the members of the Meyers and Richards families, my five siblings and assorted cousins, aunts, and uncles. Without you, there would have been no circus to run away from.

There is no MFA after my name, or before it or in the middle, for that matter. My formal writing training probably ended with the nuns by eighth grade. So, for better or worse, I have honed my skills at writing conferences and retreats.

Gratitude is due to the first of these I attended in San Miguel de Allende, Mexico, especially to Mr. Gerard Helfrich, a kind and gentle teacher who provided a lot of encouragement.

Special thanks to the *Catamaran Literary Reader* and Catherine Segurson for publishing my first piece, "Carnival

Therapy," about the three times that my mother died.

And to the San Francisco Writer's Conference who awarded me their *First Five Pages* Grand Prize for the work you are reading.

To my beta readers: Dan Balcar, Gordon Dalbey, Kenzia Drake, Anne Johnson, Chuck Kava, Victor McEvoy, Dennis Mc-Neff, Ralph Morales, Bill Perry, Joe Sheley, and Jason Strayer. Muchas gracias.

And to Nick Courtright and the folks at Atmosphere Press who thought my scribblings were worth sacrificing a tree or two for.

And finally, but certainly not least, a big hug of thanks to my wife Barbara. She read my work, offered support, and even sacrificed three Valentine's Days so I could attend writing conferences. Barbara is not the "Laura" in this book, but that's another whole story.

ABOUT ATMOSPHERE PRESS

Atmosphere Press is an independent, full-service publisher for excellent books in all genres and for all audiences. Learn more about what we do at atmospherepress.com.

We encourage you to check out some of Atmosphere's latest releases, which are available at Amazon.com and via order from your local bookstore:

Out and Back: Essays on a Family in Motion, by Elizabeth Templeman

Just Be Honest, by Cindy Yates

You Crazy Vegan: Coming Out as a Vegan Intuitive, by Jessica Ang

Detour: Lose Your Way, Find Your Path, by S. Mariah Rose

To B&B or Not to B&B: Deromanticizing the Dream, by Sue Marko

Sacred Fool, by Nathan Dean Talamentez

My Place in the Spiral, by Rebecca Beardsall

My Eight Dads, by Mark Kirby

Dinner's Ready! Recipes for Working Moms, by Rebecca Cailor

Vespers' Lament: Essays Culture Critique, Future Suffering, and Christian Salvation, by Brian Howard Luce

Without Her: Memoir of a Family, by Patsy Creedy

Emotional Liberation: Life Beyond Triggers and Trauma, by GuruMeher Khalsa

ABOUT THE AUTHOR

Nove Meyers is a fourth-generation member of a family of circus owners. He followed the family tradition by going into the food concession business and eventually owned a sizeable contract foodservice business. But before that, he spent eight years studying for the priesthood and another twenty working for the Catholic church. Recently retired, he is devoting his time to writing. He and his wife Barbara divide their time between the Pacific Northwest and Tucson, Arizona. This is his first book. You may contact Nove at: novewrites@gmail.com.

CPSIA information can be obtained
at www.ICGtesting.com
Printed in the USA
FSHW022106200122
87820FS

9 781639 889945